Math Made Easy

Extra MATH Practice

Author Sean McArdle
Consultant Alison Tribley

LONDON, NEW YORK, MUNICH, MELBOURNE, AND DELHI

DK UK
Senior Editor Deborah Lock
Art Director Martin Wilson
Publishing Director Sophie Mitchell
Pre-production Francesca Wardell
Jacket Designer Martin Wilson
US Editor Nancy Ellwood
Math Consultant Alison Tribley

DK Delhi
Editorial Monica Saigal, Tanya Desai
Design Pallavi Narain, Dheeraj Arora, Tanvi Nathyal, Jyotsna Khosla
DTP Designer Anita Yadav

First American Edition, 2013
Published in the United States by DK Publishing
375 Hudson Street, New York, New York 10014

13 14 15 16 17 10 9 8 7 6 5 4 3 2 1
001-187395-July/2013

Published in Great Britain by Dorling Kindersley Limited.

DK books are available at special discounts when purchased in bulk for sales promotions, premiums, fund-raising, or educational use.
For details, contact: DK Publishing Special Markets
375 Hudson Street, New York, New York 10014
SpecialSales@dk.com

A catalog record for this book is available from the Library of Congress
ISBN: 978-1-4654-0938-6
Printed and bound in China by L. Rex Printing Co., Ltd.

Discover more at
www.dk.com

Contents

This chart lists all the topics in the book. Once you have completed each page, stick a star in the correct box below.

Read and write 1, 2, and 3

Write the number.

1

Write the word.

one

Write the number.

2

Write the word.

two

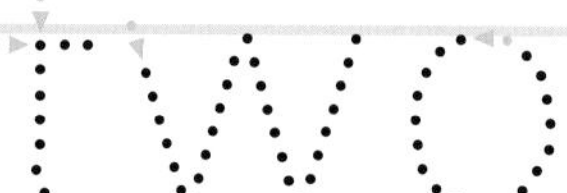

Write the number.

3

Write the word.

three

Write the number.

4 4

Write the word.

four four

Write the number.

5 5

Write the word.

five five

How many?

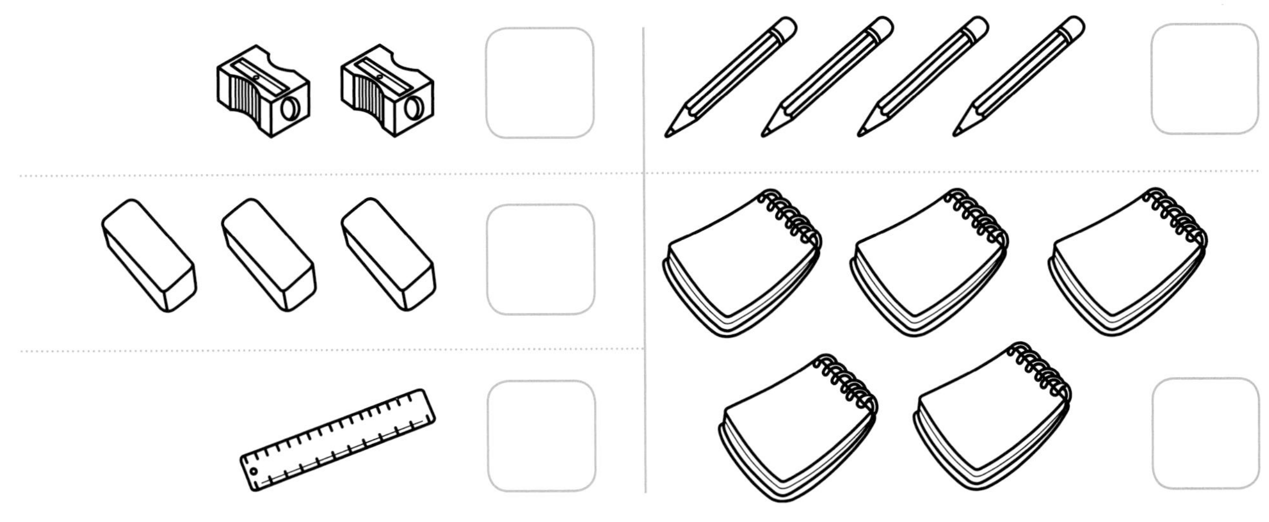

Circles and ovals

This is a circle.

Draw a circle around each object.

Draw some circles of your own.

These are ovals. An oval is egg-shaped.
An oval is like a squashed circle.

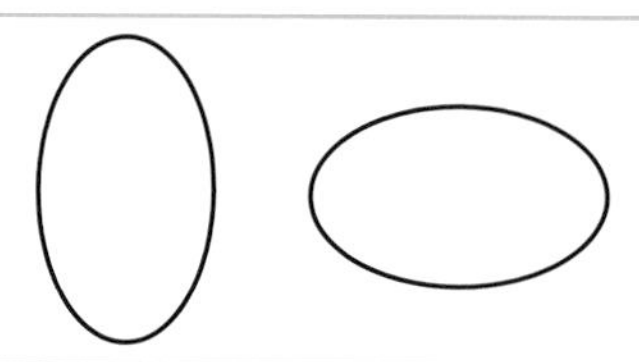

Draw an oval around each object.

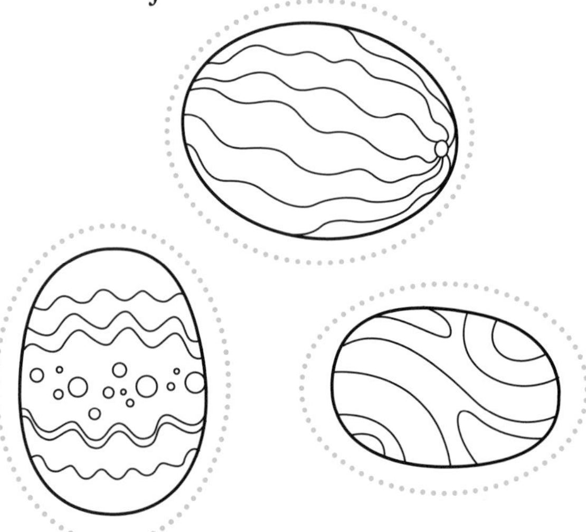

Draw some ovals of your own.

Circle the animal that is the same.

Counting 1 to 5

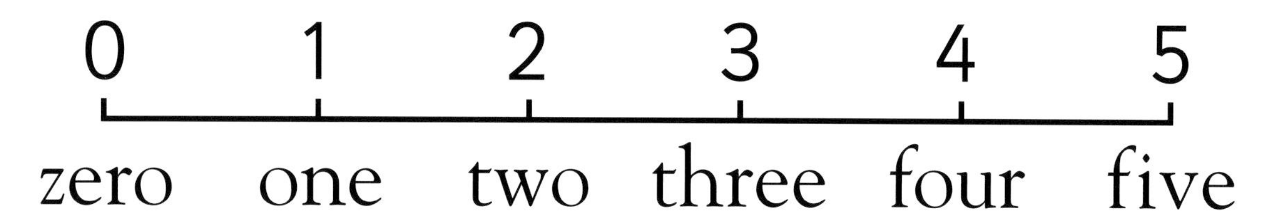

Count the objects in each group. Then write down the number that is **one more** than the group. Write the number and the word.

Draw **one more** in each group.

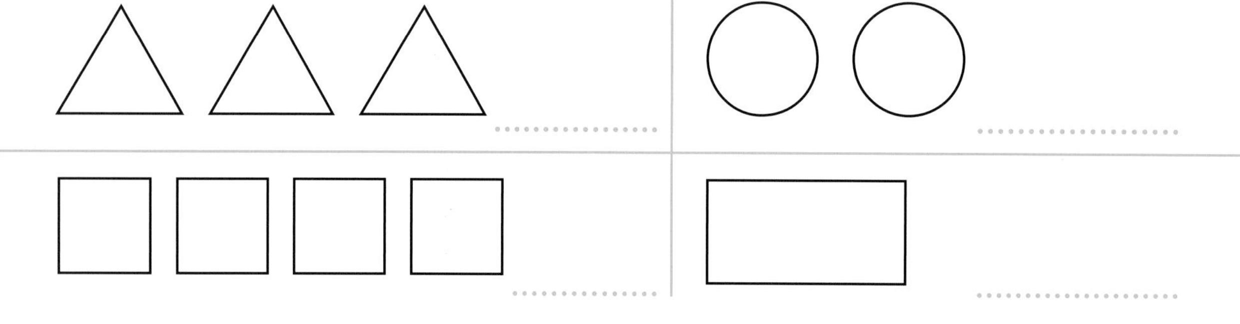

How many objects in each group or set? Write the number in the box.

Triangles

Triangles have three straight sides and three corners. 

Circle the triangles.

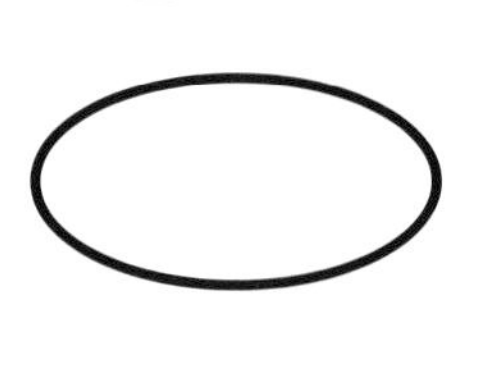  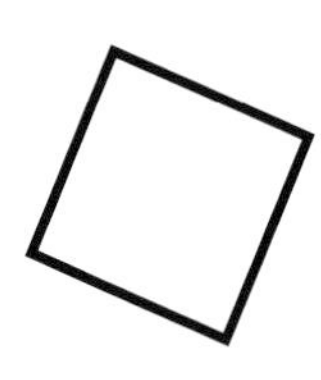 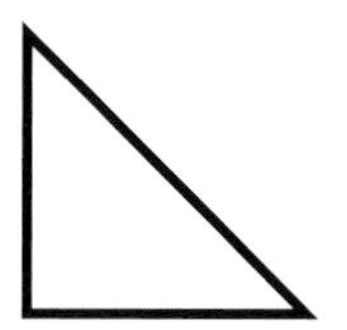 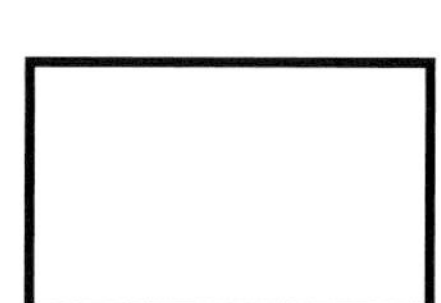

 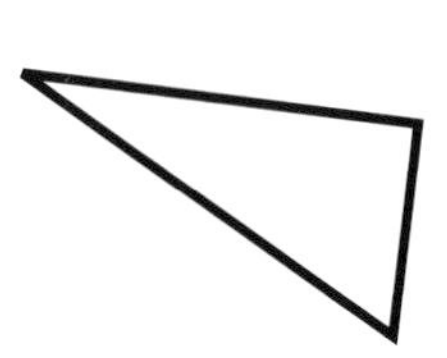 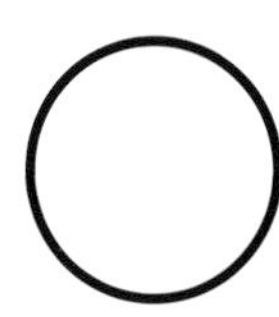 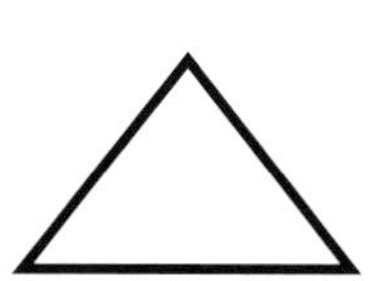 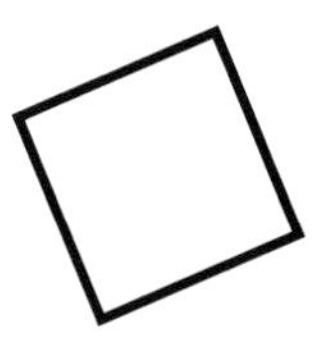

Connect the triangles that are exactly the same.

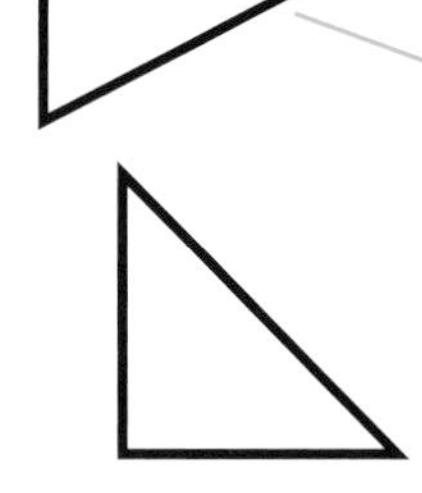

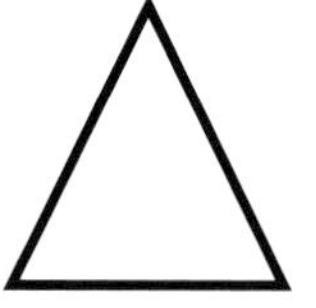

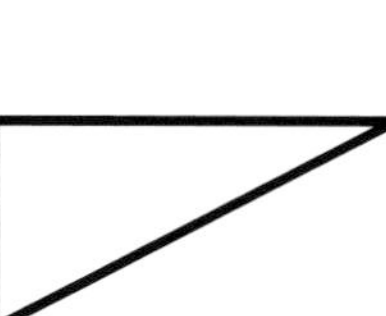

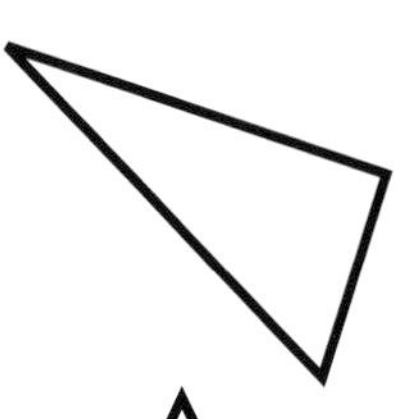

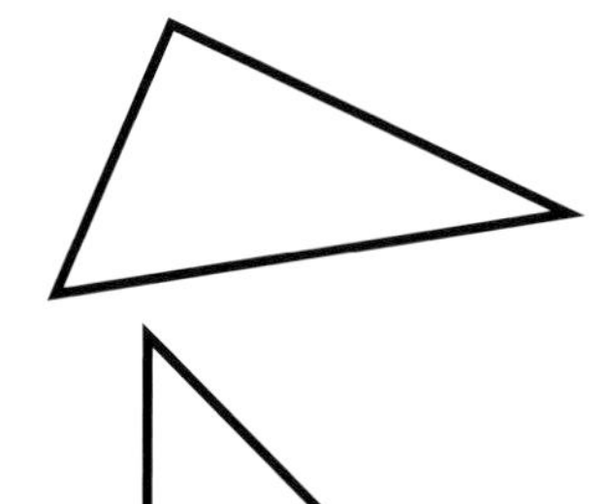

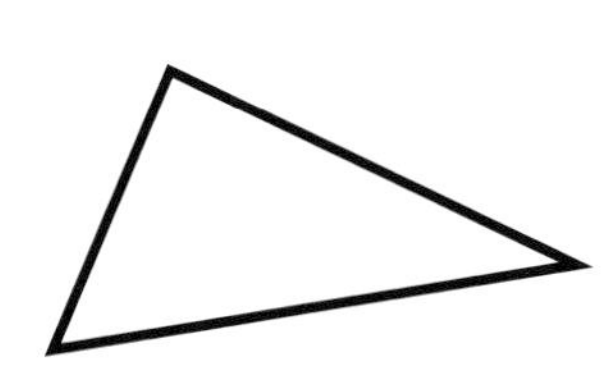

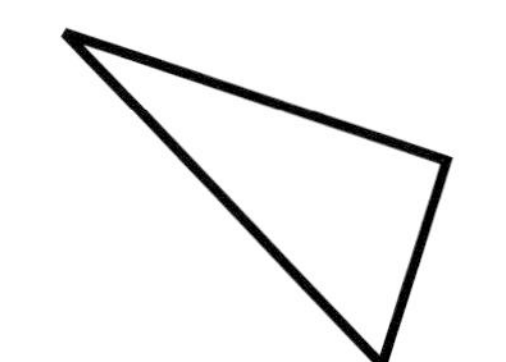

Not the same, different

Circle the fruit that is **not the same**.

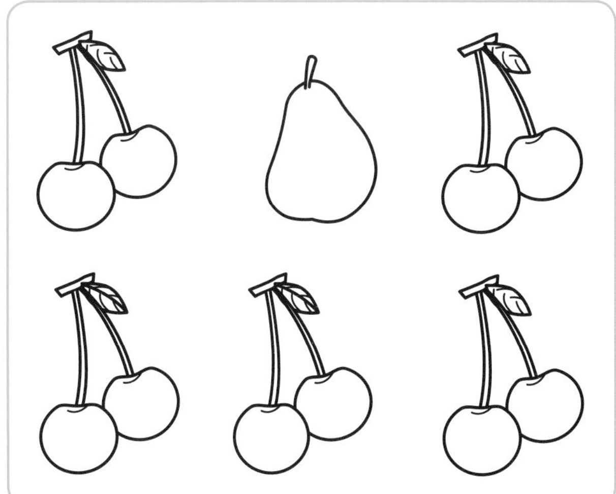

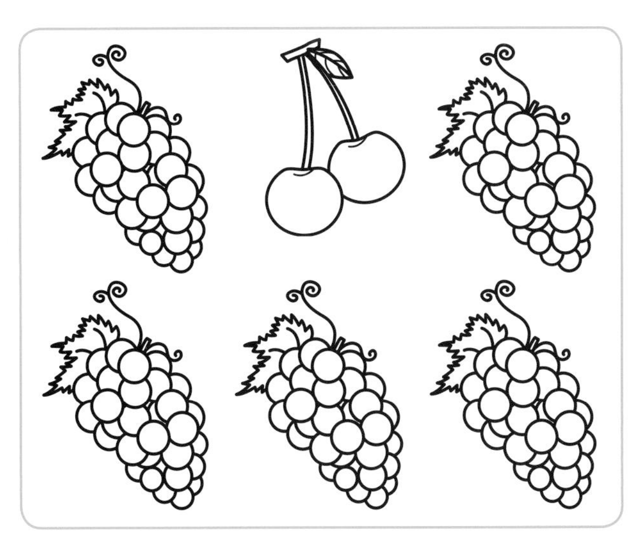

Color and pattern

Color the ovals green.

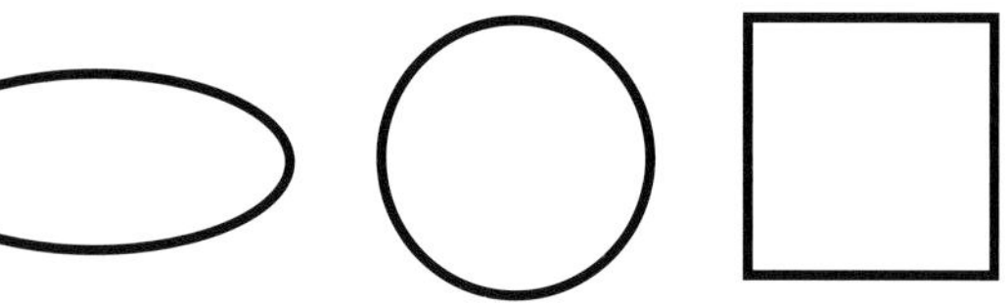

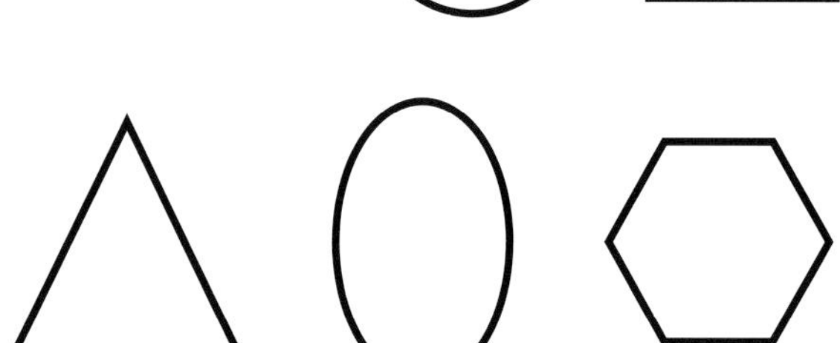

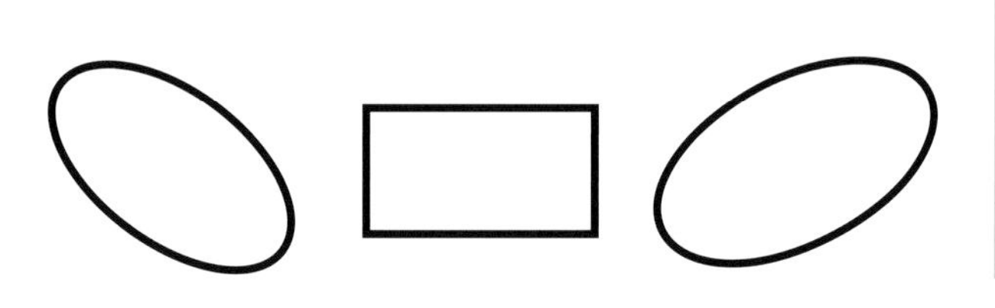

Color the triangles blue.

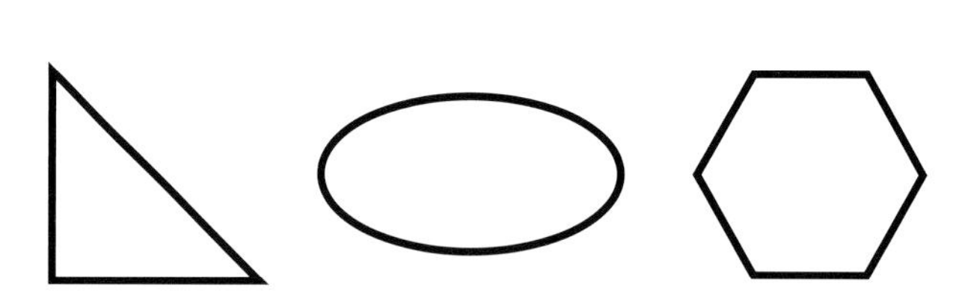

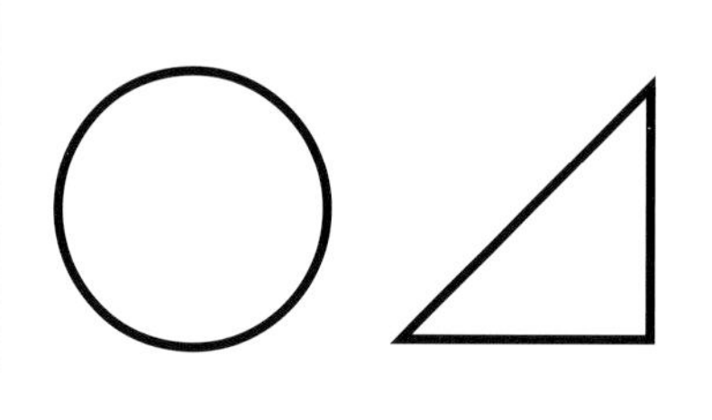

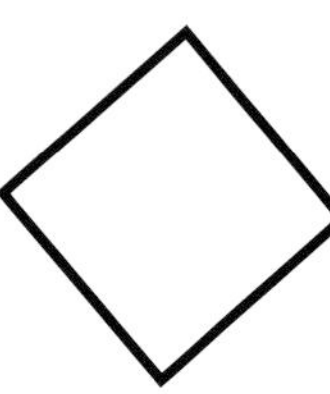

Draw the next shape.

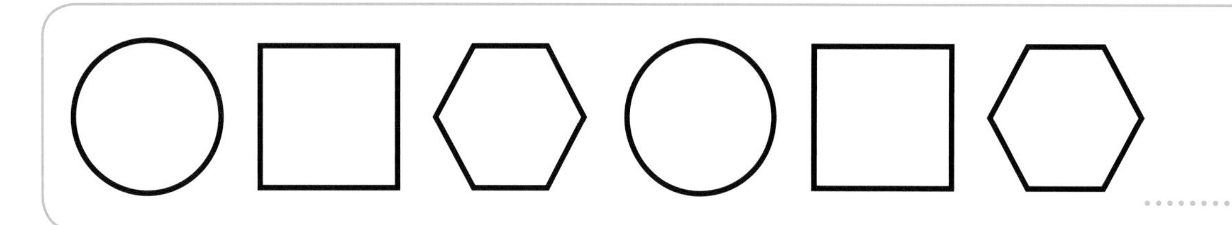

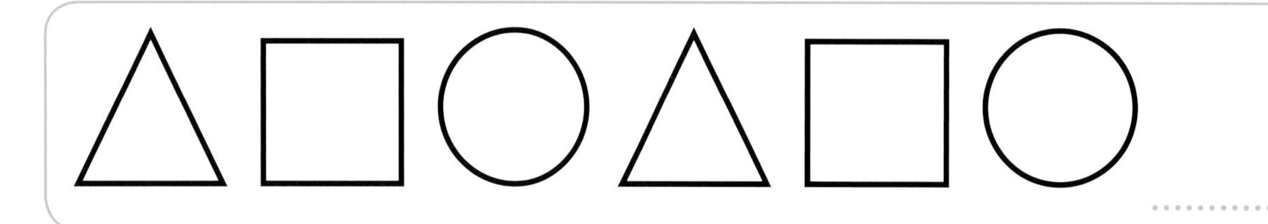

Connect the matching numbers, pictures, and words.

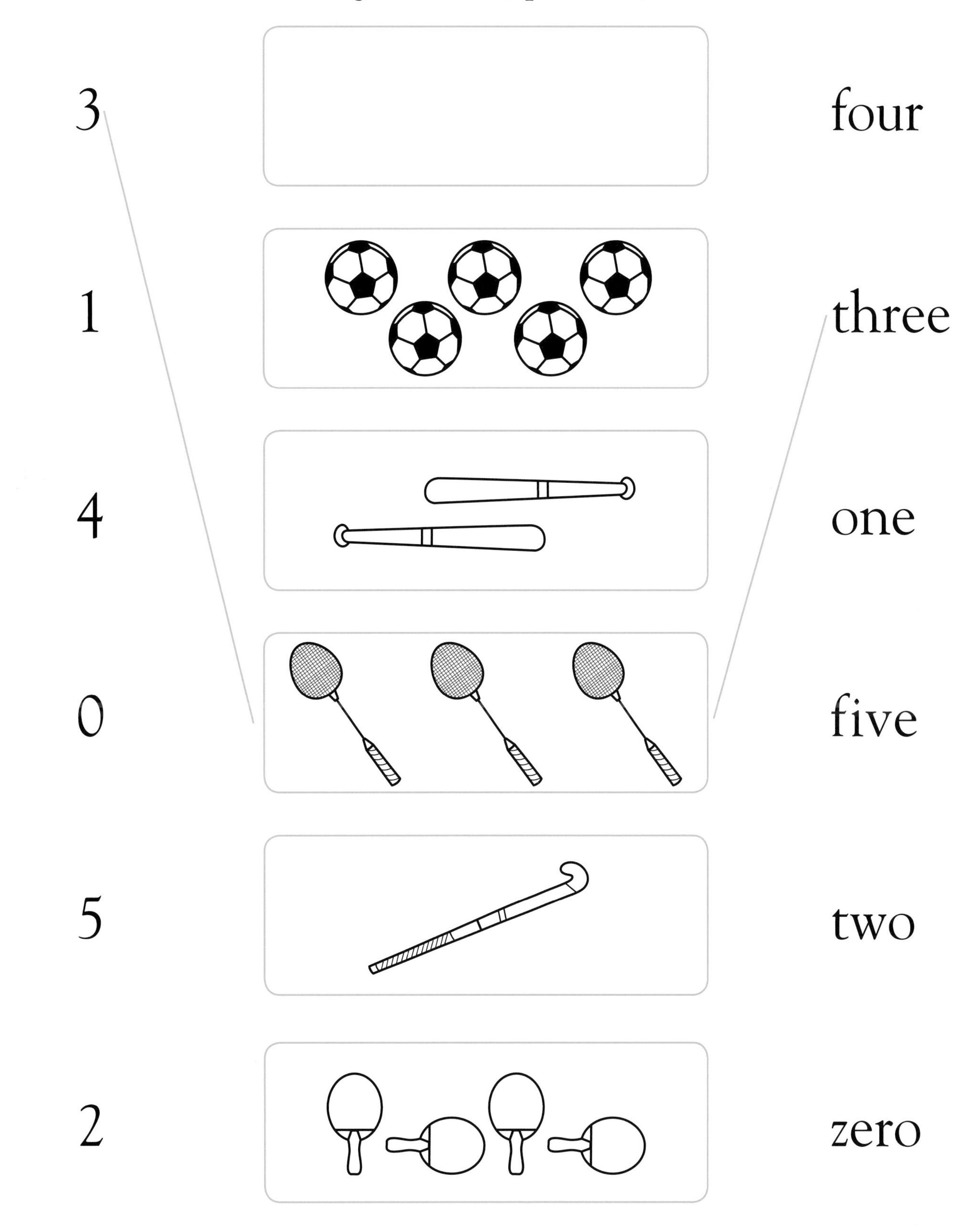

Which has more?

In each row, cross out (X) the group that has more.

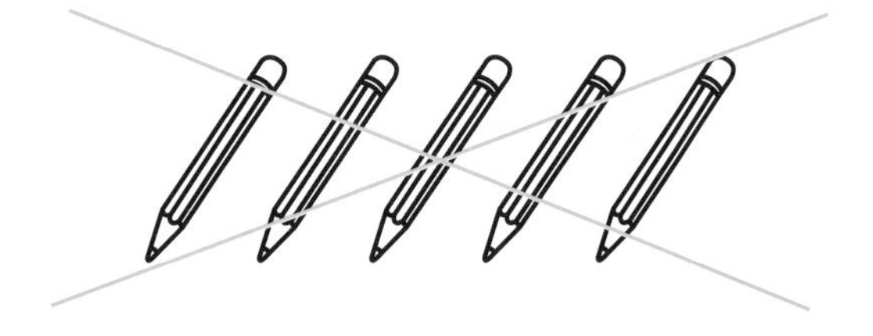

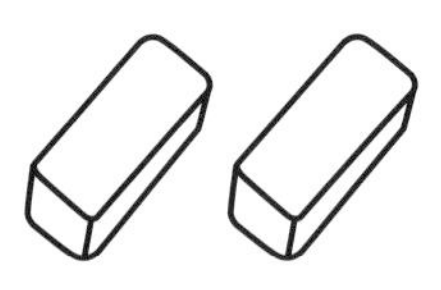

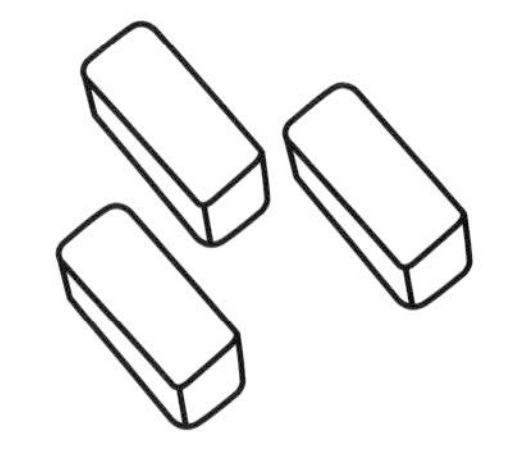

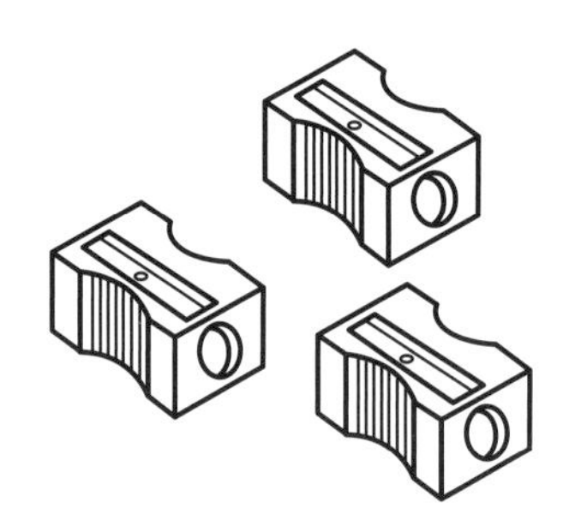

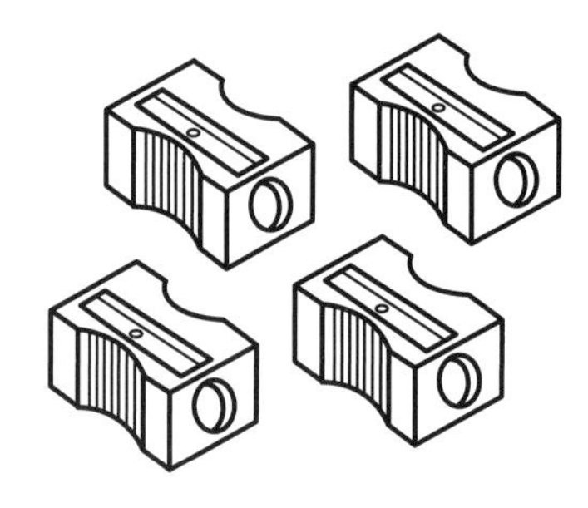

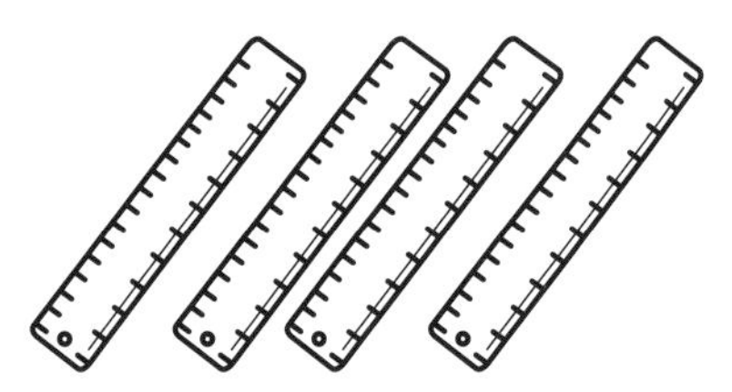

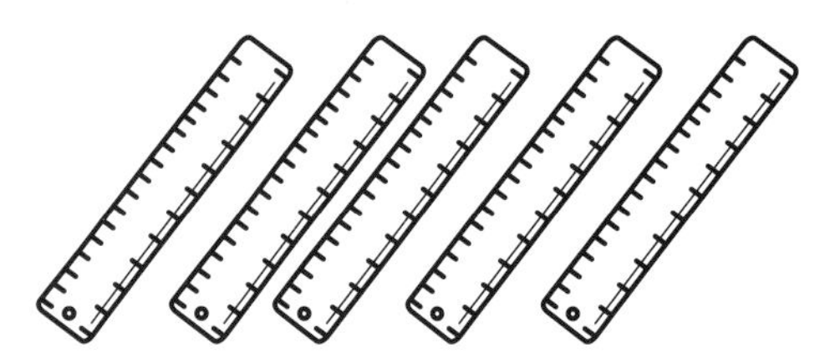

Draw the flowers and write the numbers to complete each sentence.

1 more than 3 is 4

1 more than 1 is

2 more than 1 is

2 more than 2 is

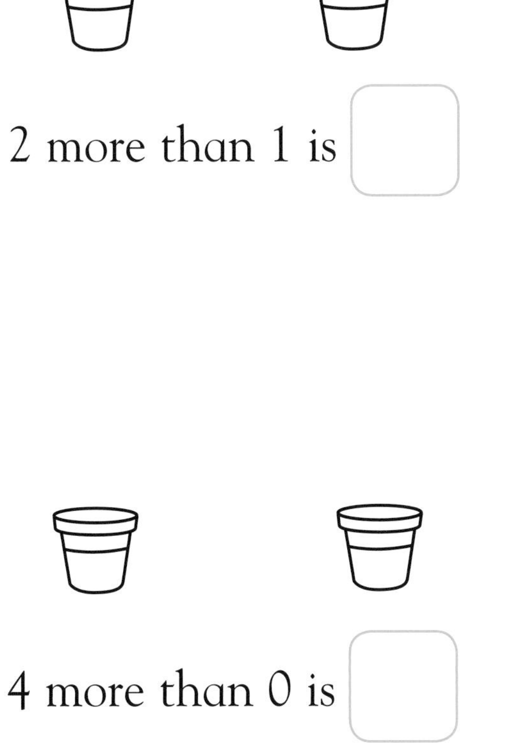

4 more than 0 is

3 more than 1 is

Cross out (X) all the triangles below.

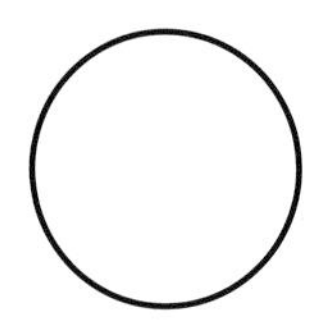 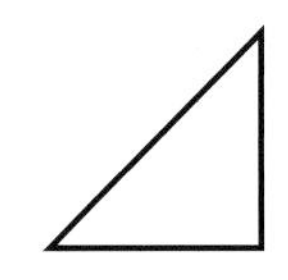 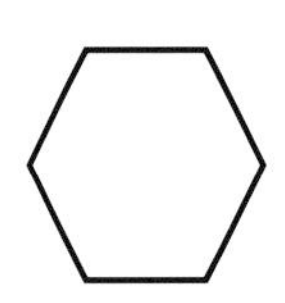 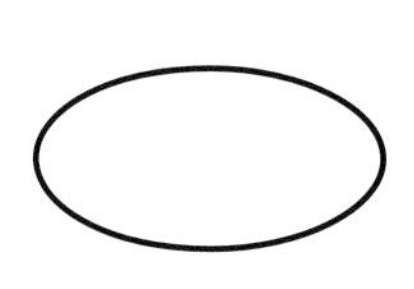 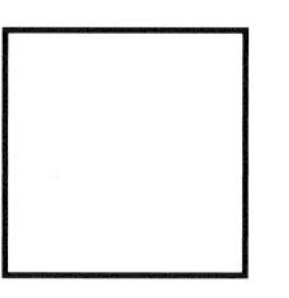 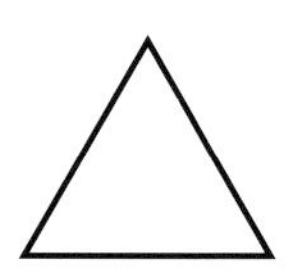

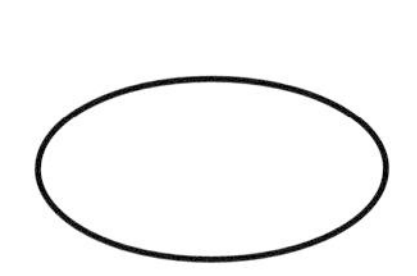 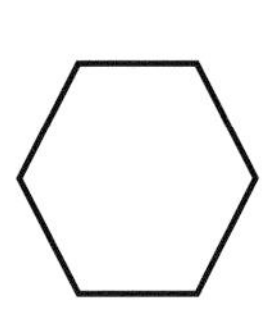 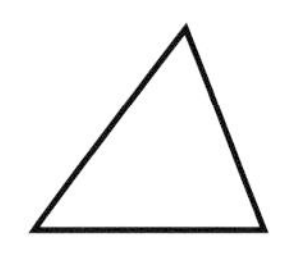 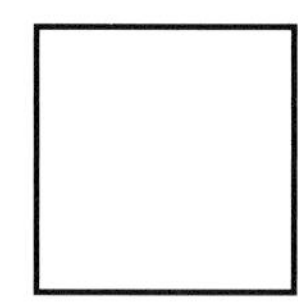 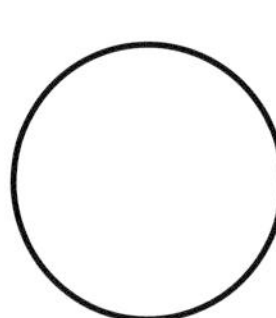 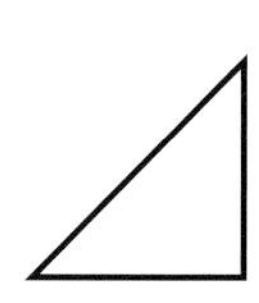

Write 1 more than each number.

4  3  1 

0  2 

How many?

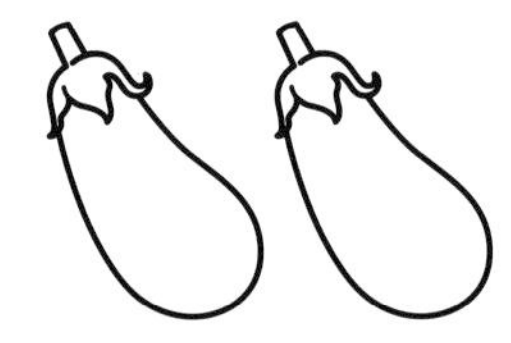  eggplants

  tomatoes

Connect the word to the number.

one	3
three	5
five	1

Connect the name to the shape.

oval

circle

triangle

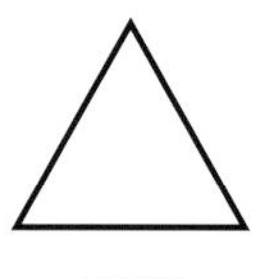

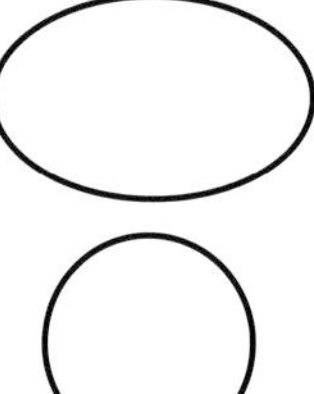

Circle the vegetables that are **not the same** as the carrot.

Draw a smiley face ☺ next to the group that has more.

What is 1 more than each number?

Write the answer.

1 more than 3 is 

2 is one more than 

Write the number.

6 6

Write the word.

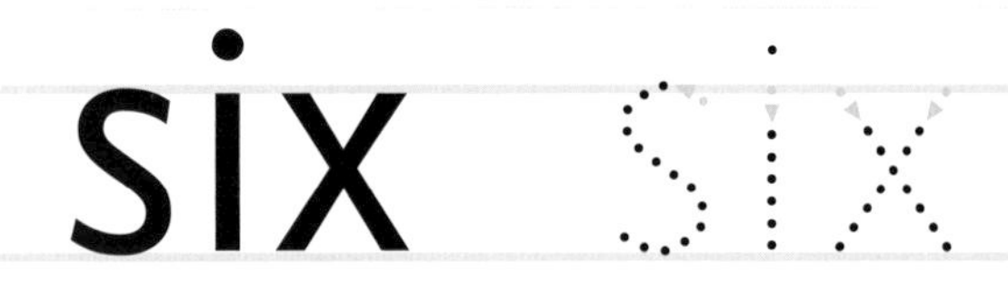

Draw 6 circles.

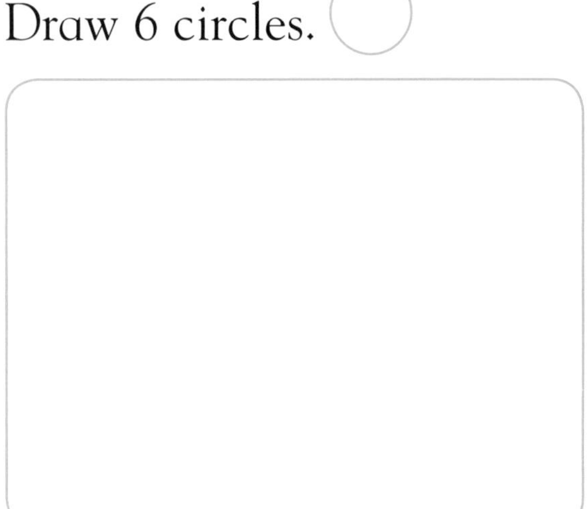

Draw six ovals.

Draw 6 squares.

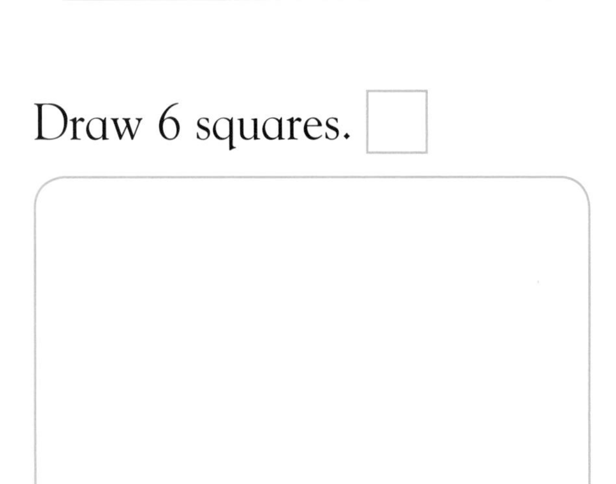

Draw six triangles.

Write the number.

7 7

Write the word.

seven seven

Cross out (X) the groups with 7 animals.

Squares

This is a square. A square has four sides of the same length and four right angles.

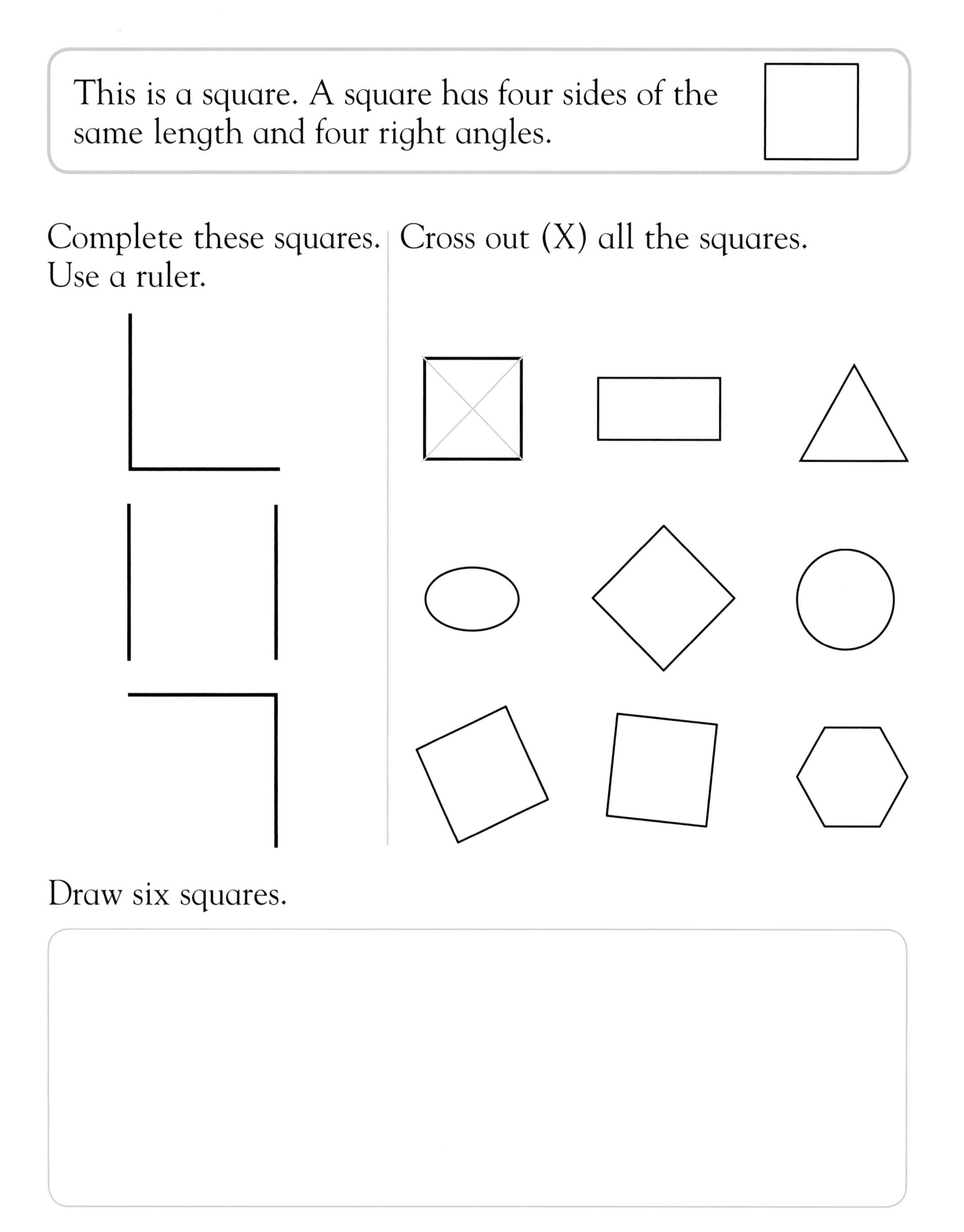

Complete these squares. Use a ruler.

Cross out (X) all the squares.

Draw six squares.

Draw the other half of each object.

Read, write, and draw 8

Write the number.

8 8

Write the word.

eight eight

Count the objects and write the answers in numbers and words.

Write the number.

9 9

Write the word.

nine nine

Circle the groups with 9 items.

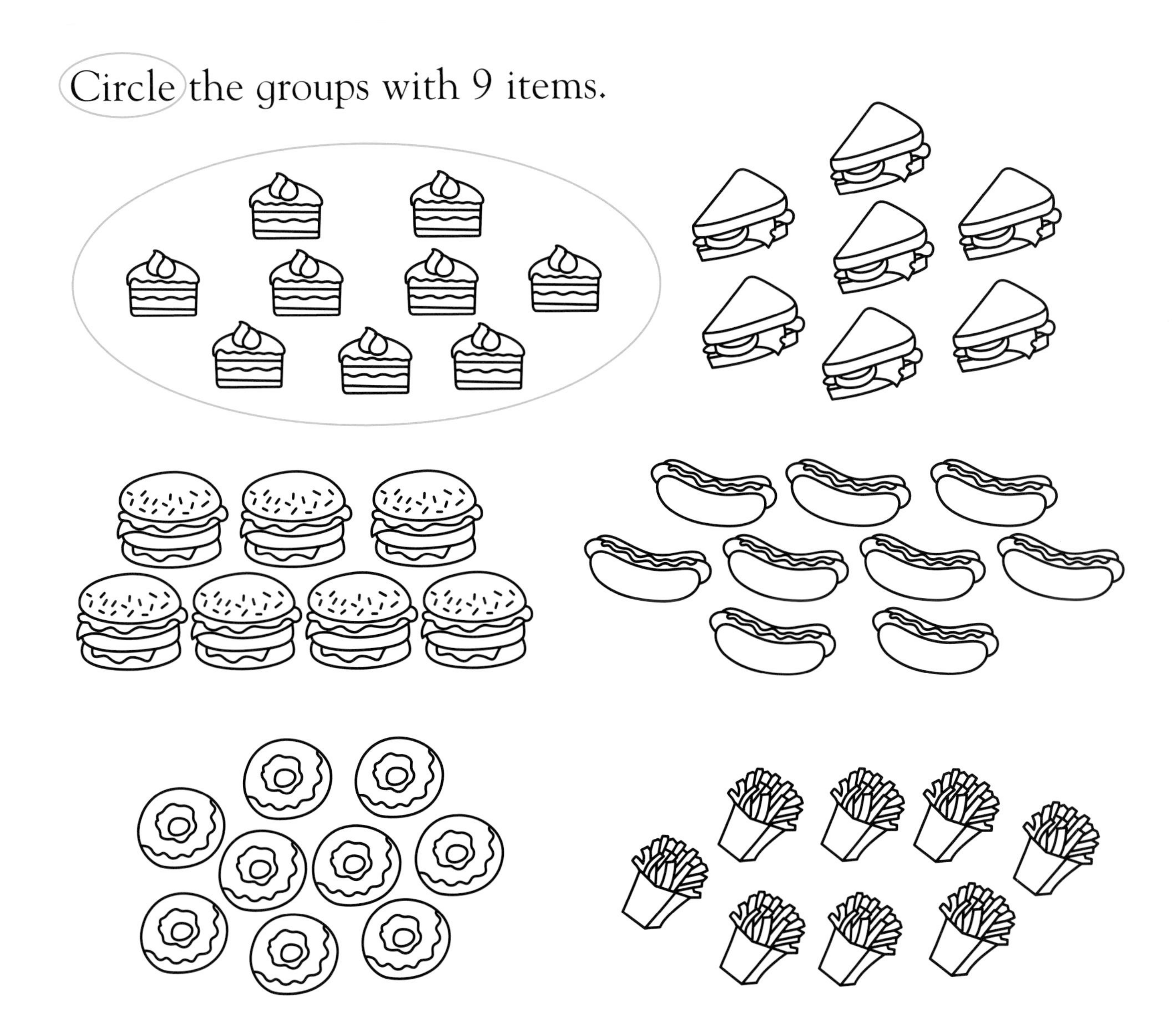

Read, write, and draw 10

Write the number.

10 10

Write the word.

ten ten

Draw 10 circles.

Draw ten triangles.

How many toes are on two feet?

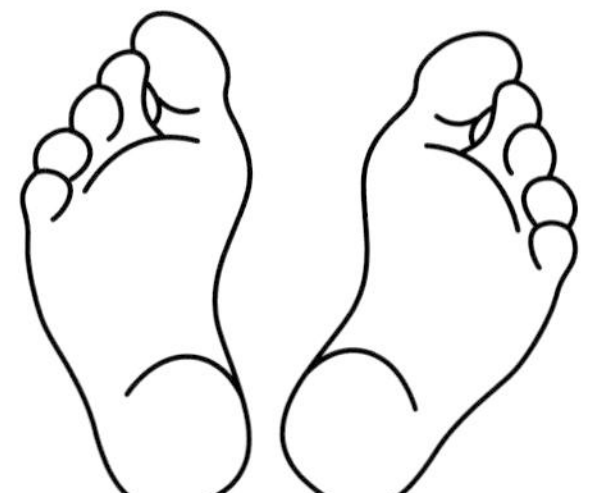

Draw two hands.

This is a special sign **+**. It means **add**.
We can also say **plus**.

What is the answer?

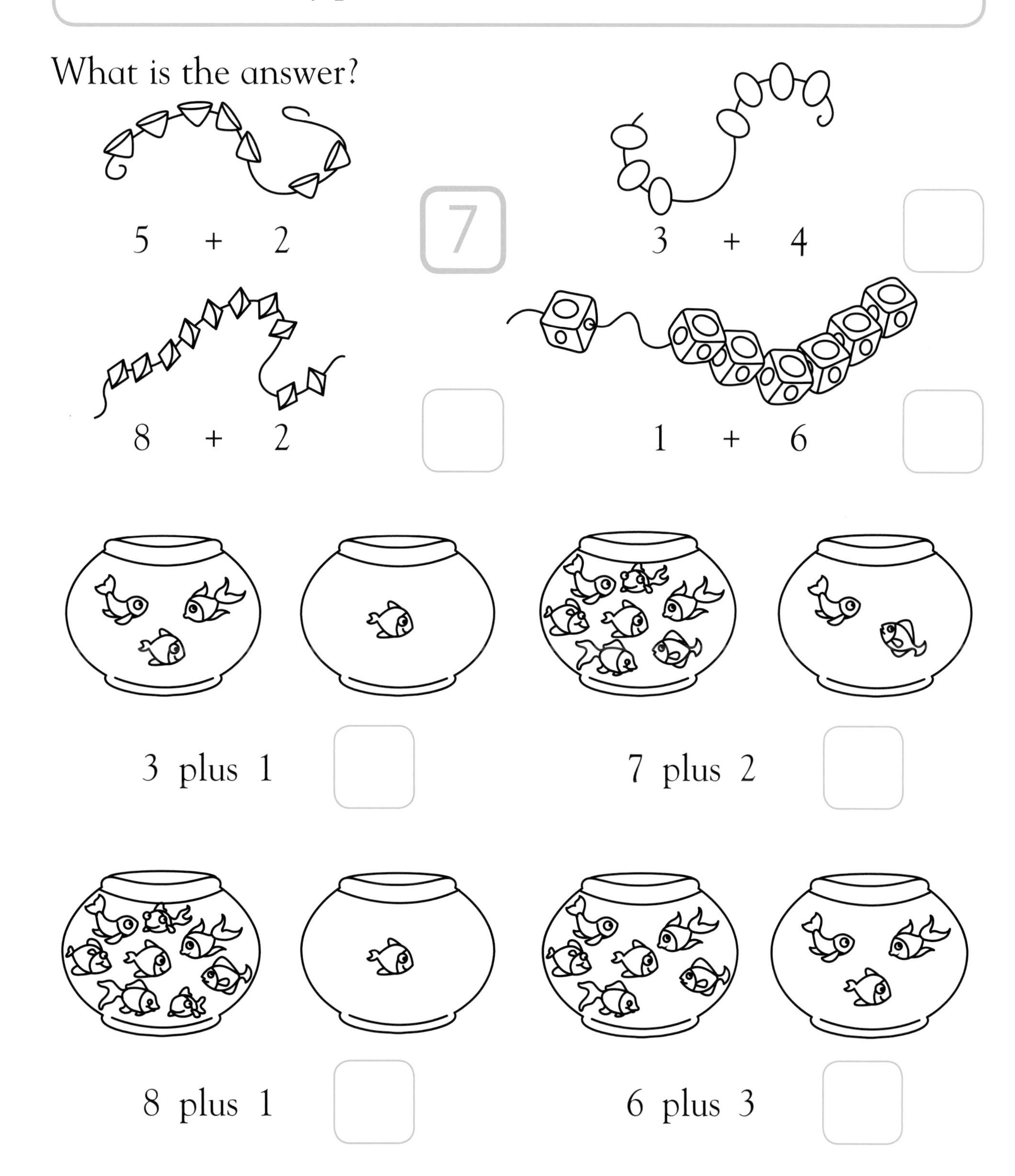

Taking away

This is a special sign –. It means **minus**, **subtract**, and **take away**.

Draw the apples and write the numbers that make each sentence true.

4 is one less than 5

7 is one less than ....

8 is one less than ....

3 is one less than ....

What is the answer?

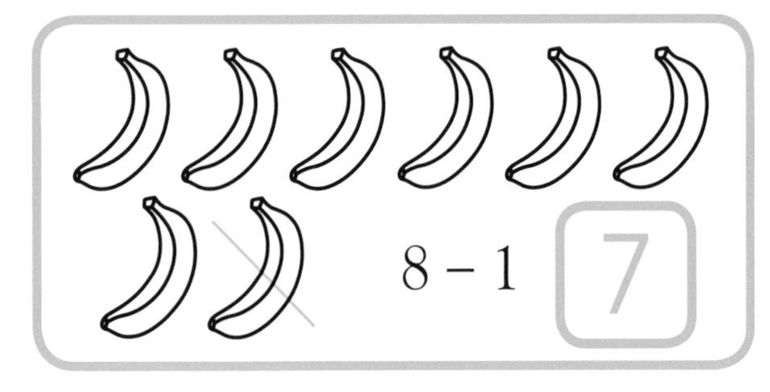

$8 - 1$ 7

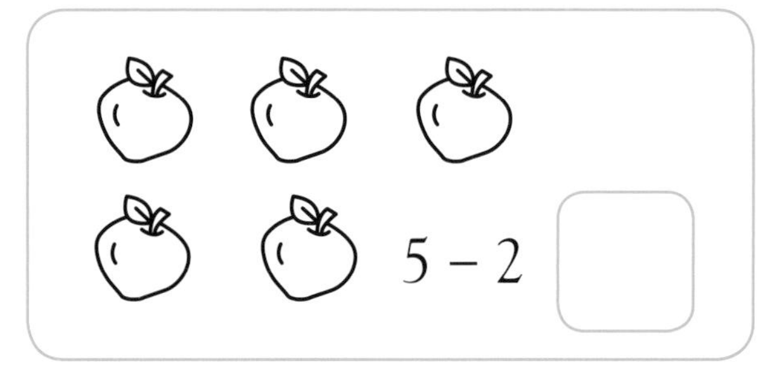

$5 - 2$

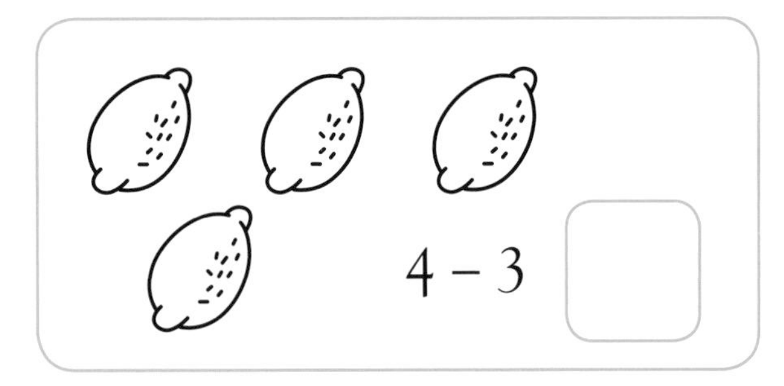

$4 - 3$

$9 - 4$

Count up.

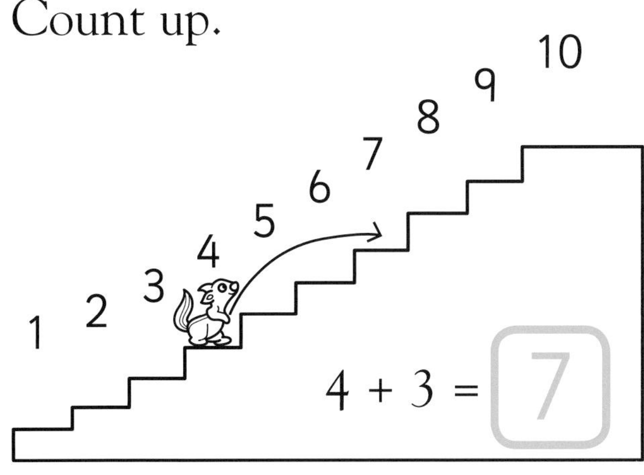

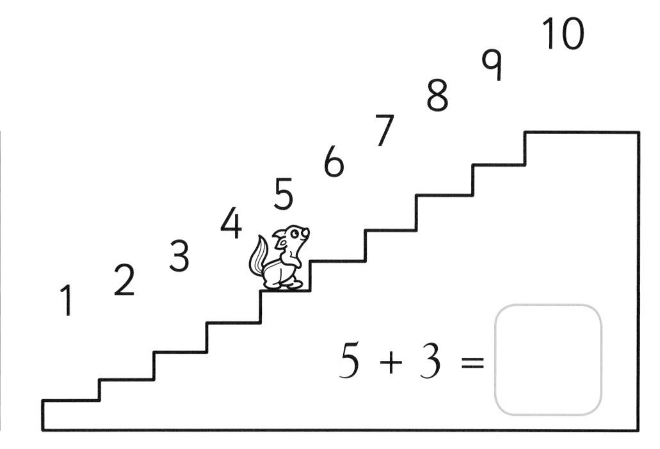

Count down.

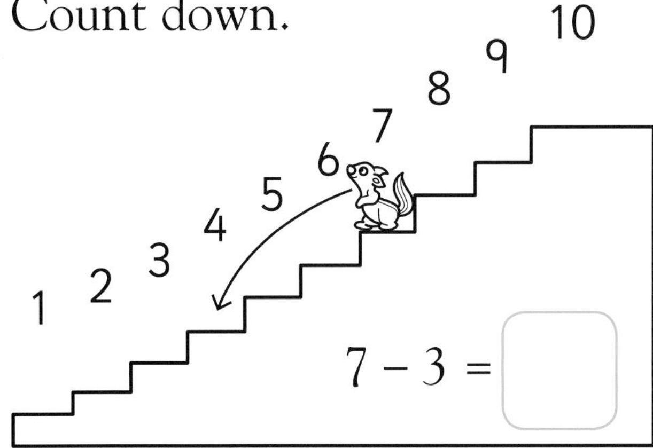

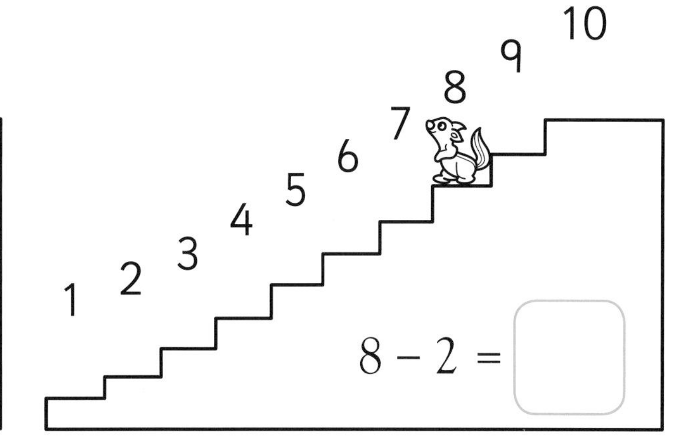

Write the missing numbers in the boxes.
Use the number line below to help you.

5 + 5 = 10

9 – 4 =

10 – 1 =

6 + 4 =

9 + 1 =

8 – 6 =

0 1 2 3 4 5 6 7 8 9 10

Here are some 4-sided shapes.

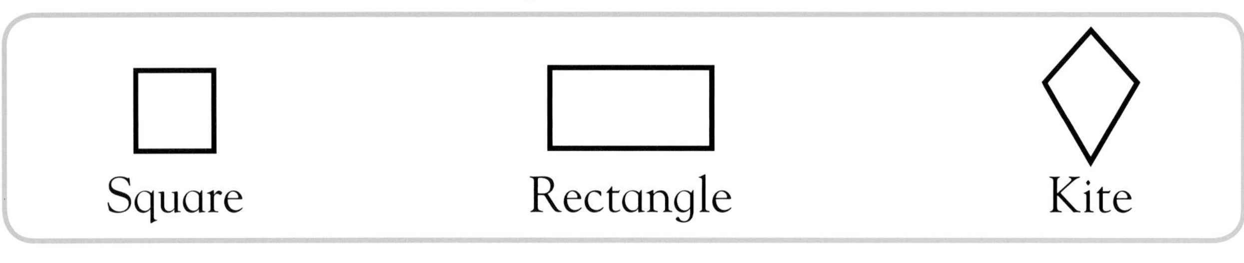

Cross out (X) the squares.

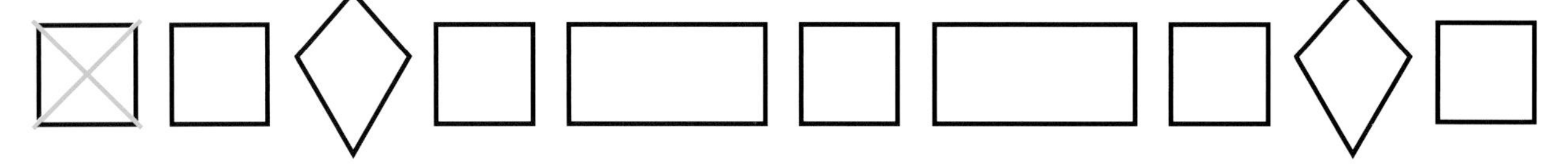

Cross out (X) the rectangles.

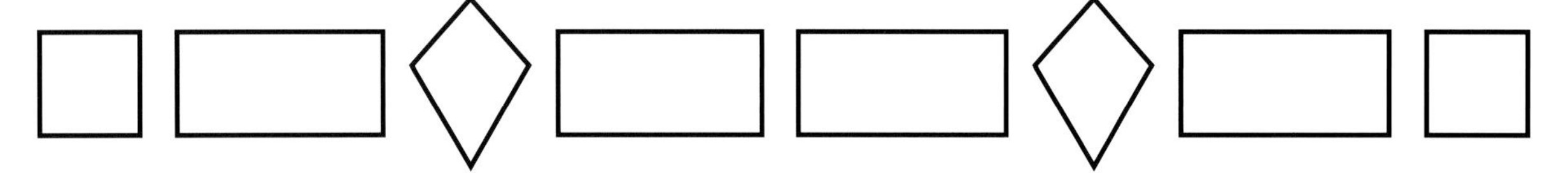

Cross out (X) the kites.

Cross out (X) the rectangle shapes.

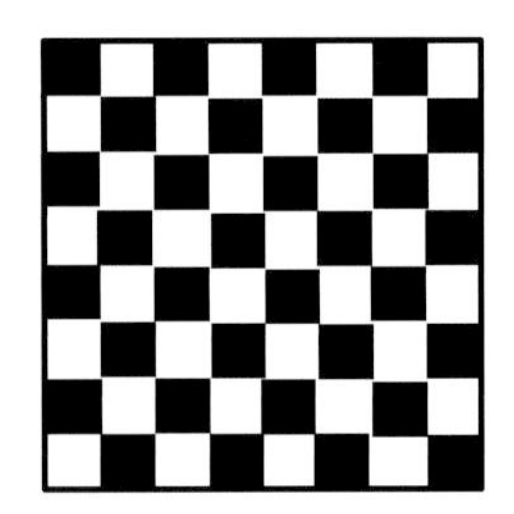

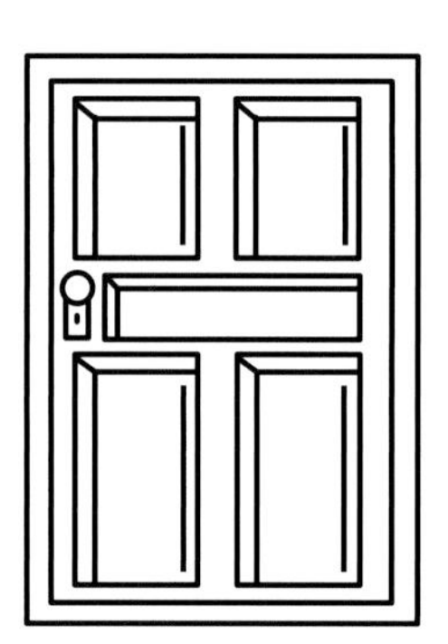

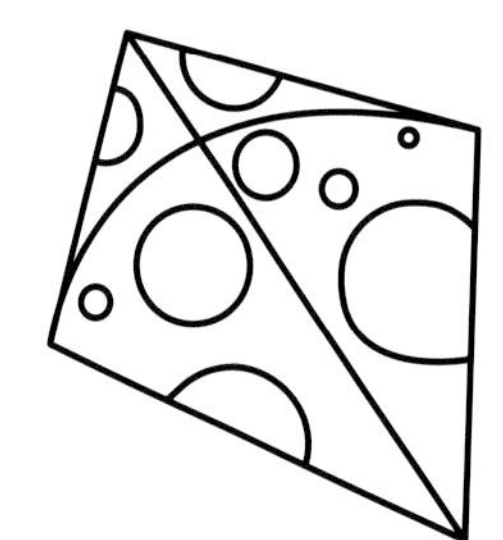

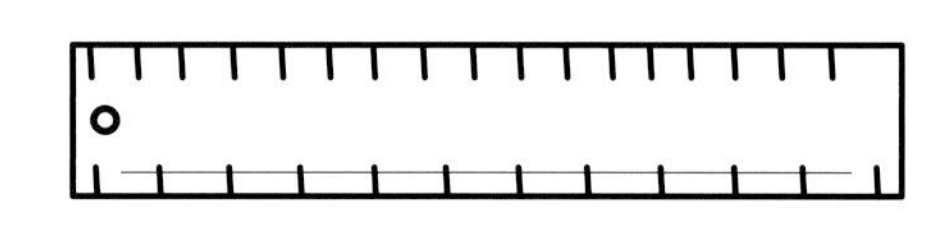

Connect the dots to make a number or shape.

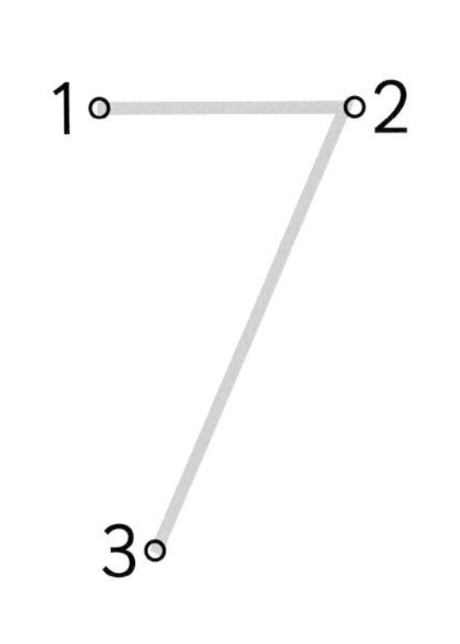

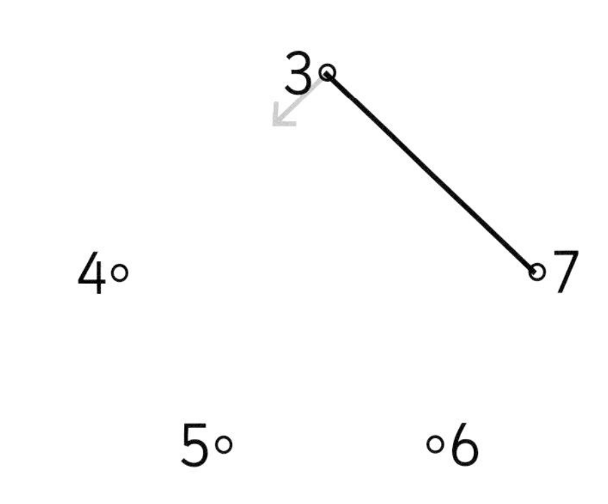

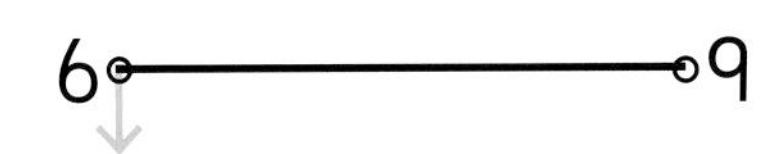

7 8

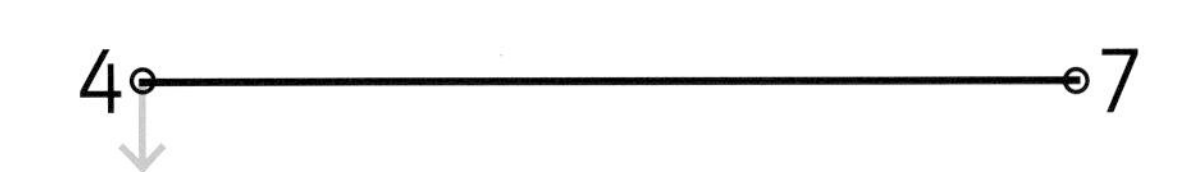

5 6

2

3 4

1

1

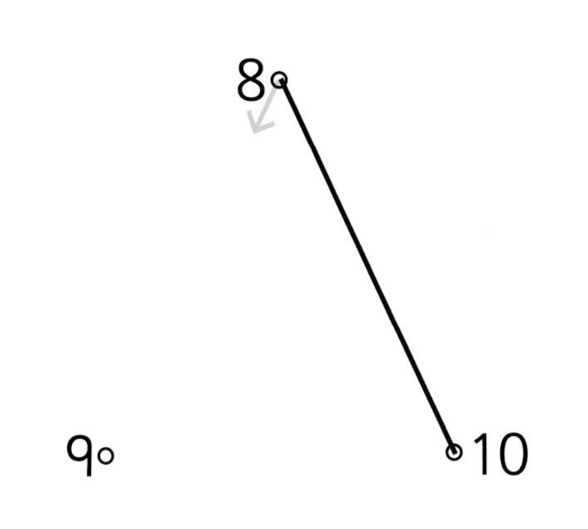

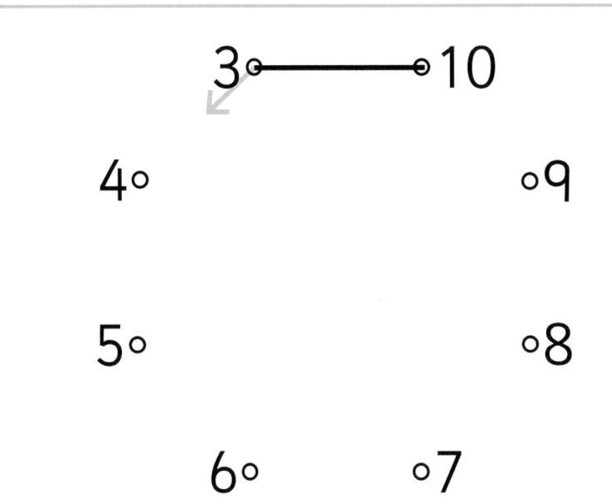

Connect the word to the number.

seven	6
nine	10
eight	9
six	7
ten	8

Draw the other half.

Write the answers.

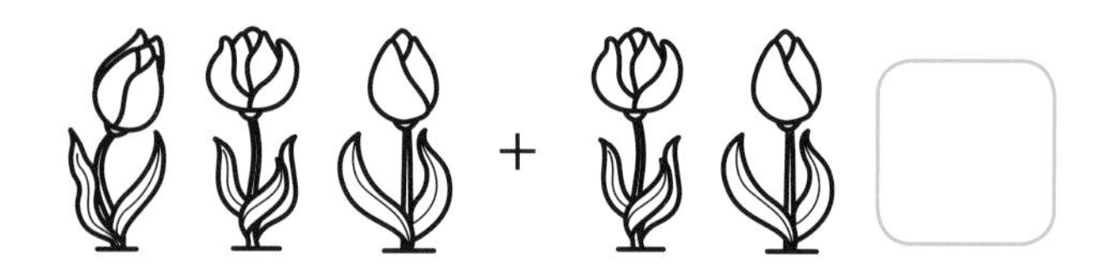

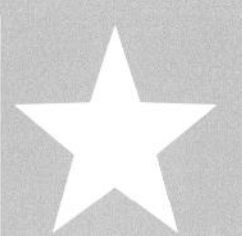

How many candies? Draw the candies in the jar.

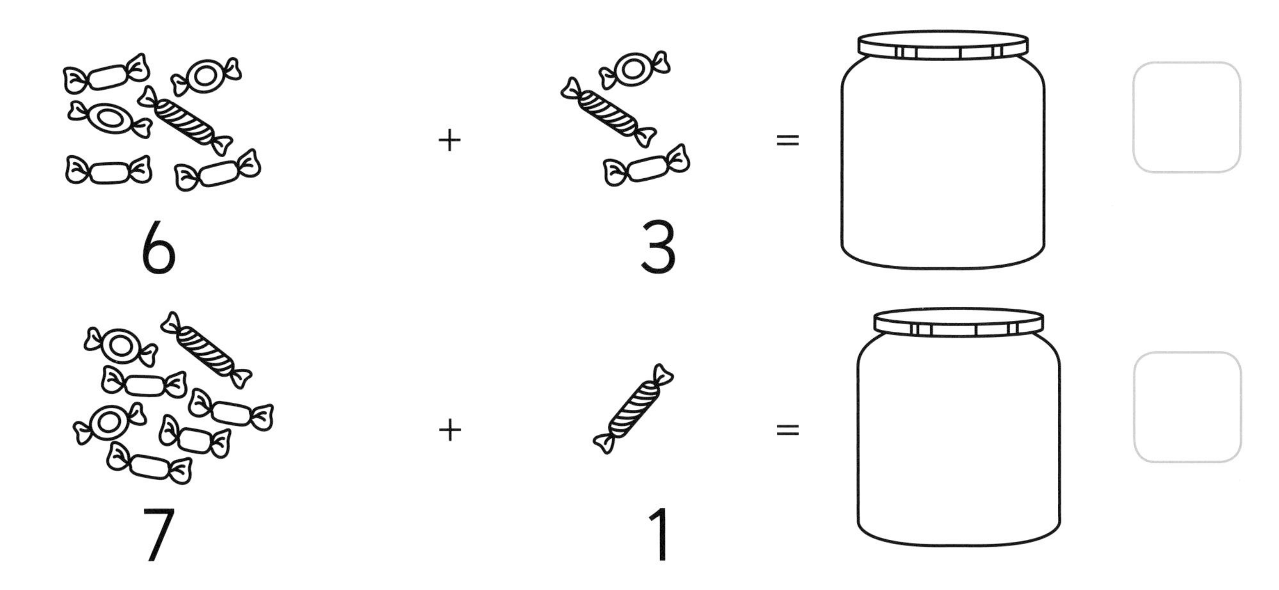

Write the answers. Use the number line below to help you.

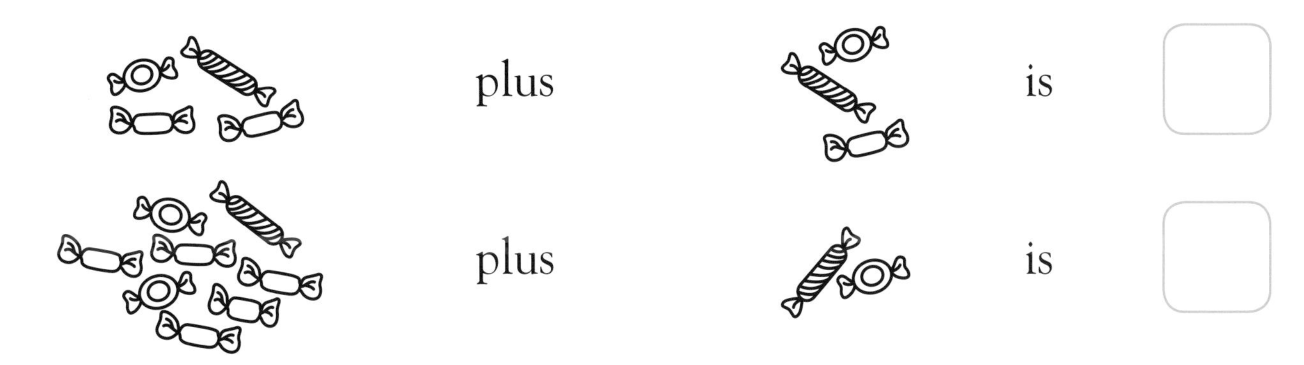

Write the answers. Use the number line below to help you.

Four add four is ☐ Nine plus one is ☐

Eight plus one is ☐ Two add three is ☐

0 1 2 3 4 5 6 7 8 9 10

Count 11, 12, and 13

Write the number.

11 11

Write the word.

eleven eleven

Write the number.

12 12

Write the word.

twelve twelve

Write the number.

13 13

Write the word.

thirteen thirteen

Write the number.

14 14

Write the word.

fourteen fourteen

Write the number.

15 15

Write the word.

fifteen fifteen

How many?

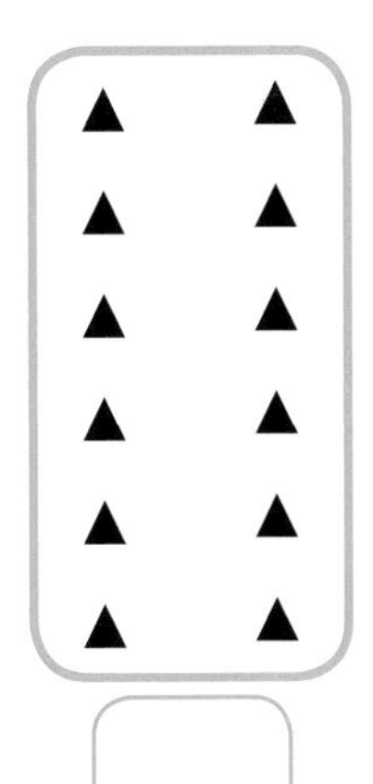

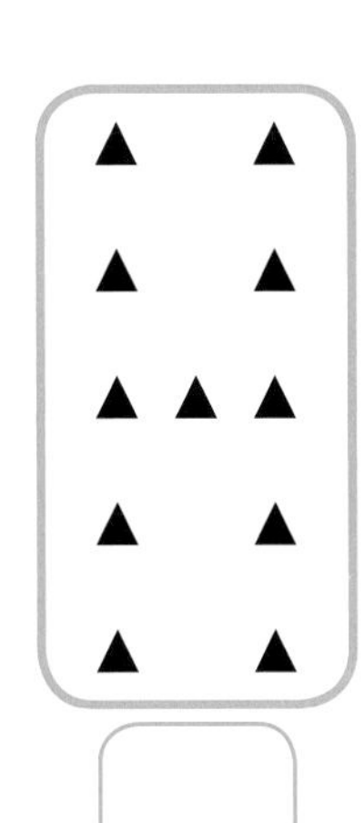

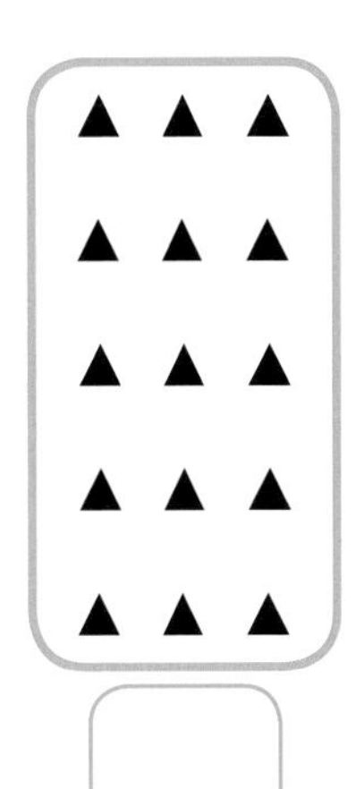

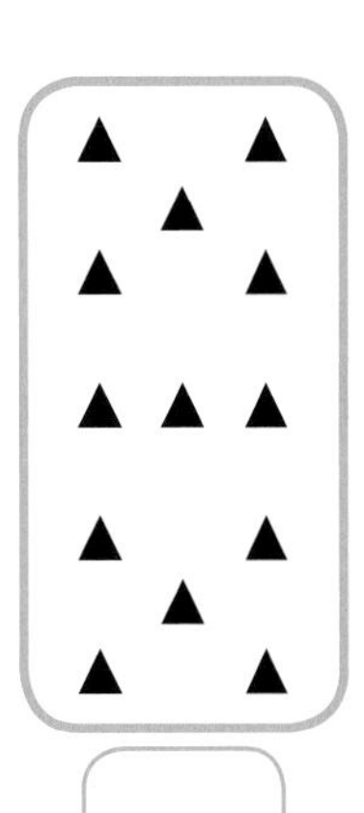

Sorting objects into sets

Connect all the animals that are the same.

Connect all the shapes that are the same.

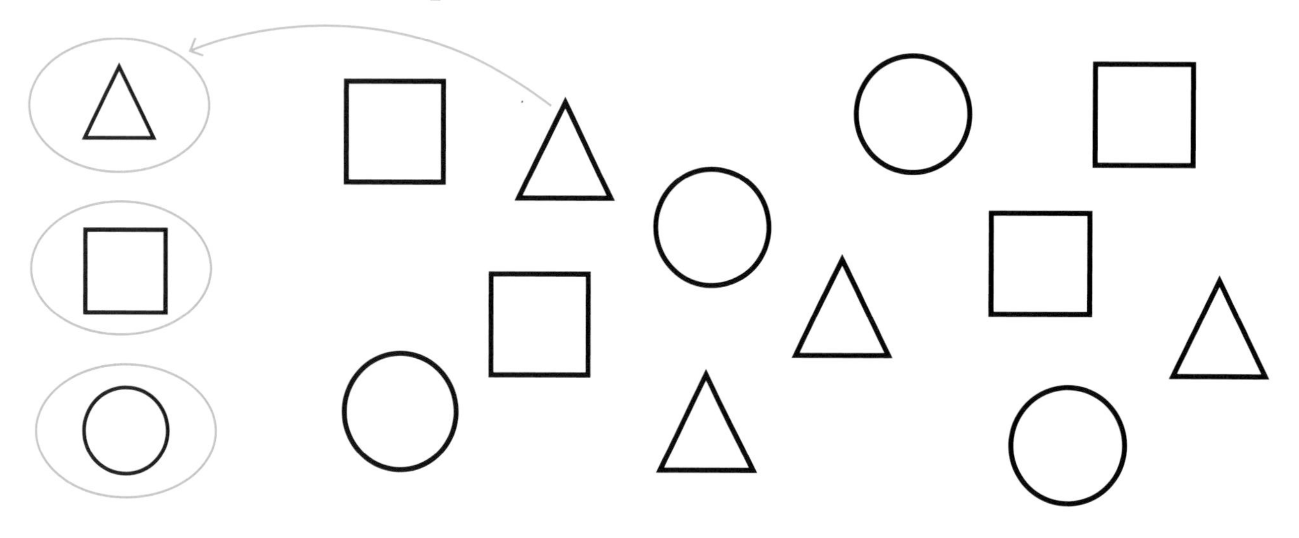

Connect all the fruits that are the same.

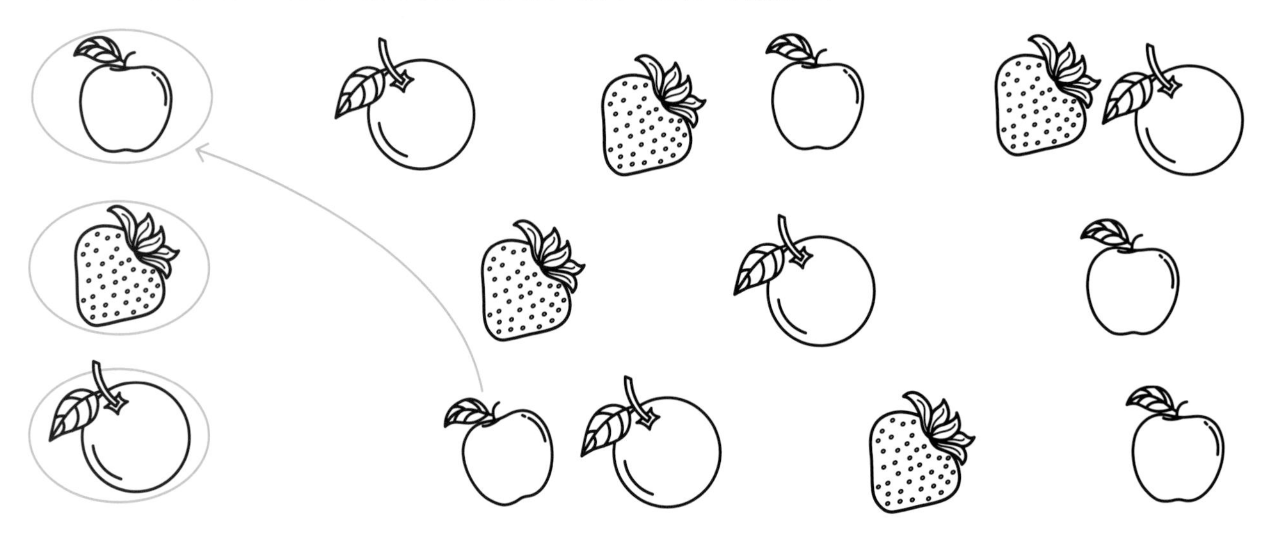

Continue each pattern.

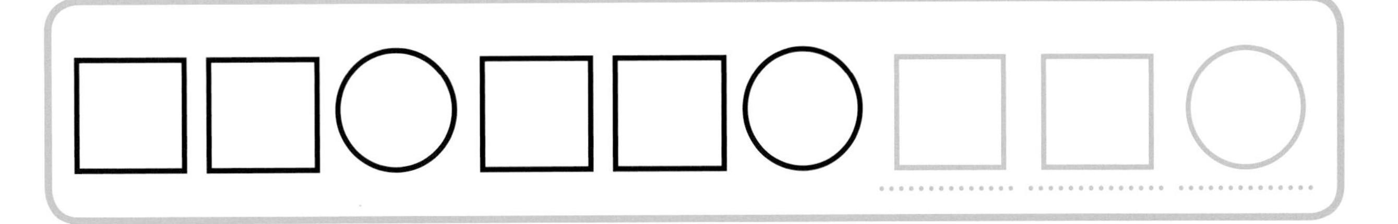

2 4 1 1 2 4 1 1 ....

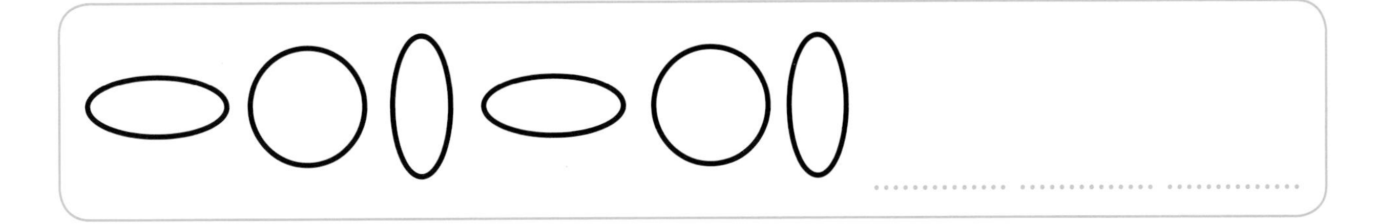

3 5 7 3 5 7 ....

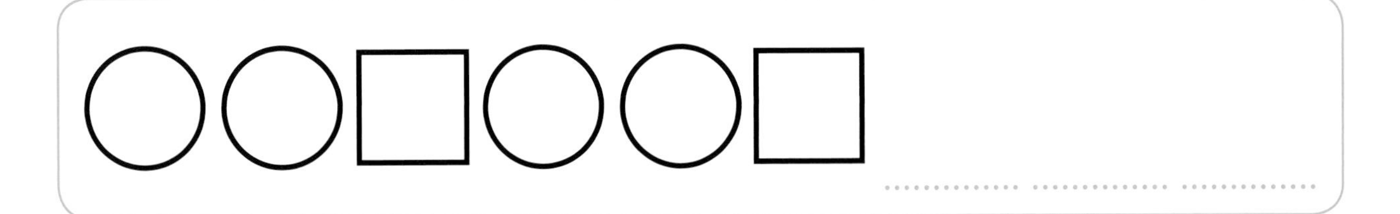

0 1 2 3 4 5 6 7 8 9 10

What is 2 less and 2 more than each number?

Write the answer. Use the number line.

12 + 2 ☐ 6 add 2  14 plus 2 

15 − 2 ☐ 14 subtract 2  8 minus 2 

11 12 13 14 15 16 17 18 19 20

What makes 5?

3 + 2 9 - ☐

0 + ☐ 5 - ☐

What makes 6?

2 + ☐ 8 - ☐

5 + ☐ 9 - ☐

What makes 7?

4 + ☐ 8 - ☐

5 + ☐ 10 - ☐

What makes 8?

3 + ☐ 9 - ☐

2 + ☐ 10 - ☐

What makes 9?

3 + ☐ 10 - ☐

6 + ☐ 9 - ☐

What makes 10?

6 + ☐ 13 - ☐

1 + ☐ 15 - ☐

Count 16, 17, and 18

Write the number.

16 16

Write the word.

sixteen sixteen

Write the number.

17 17

Write the word.

seventeen seventeen

Write the number.

18 18

Write the word.

eighteen eighteen

Write the number.

19 19

Write the word.

nineteen nineteen

Write the number.

20 20

Write the word.

twenty twenty

How many?

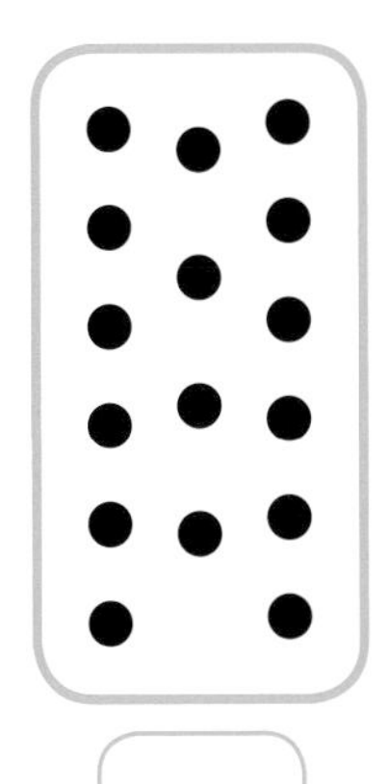 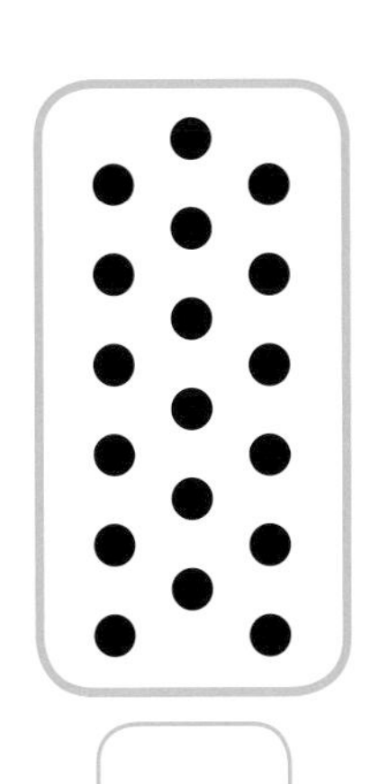  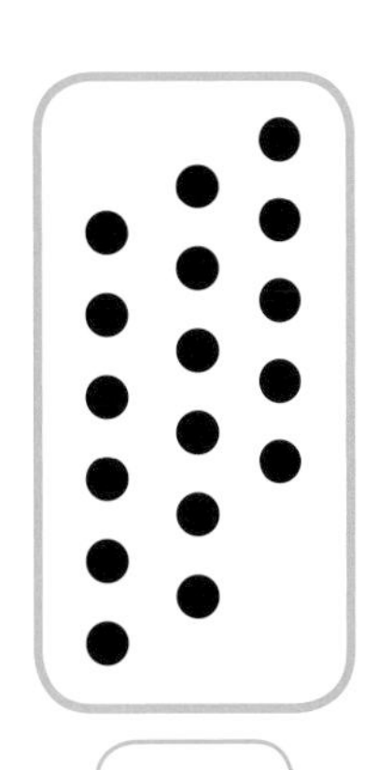 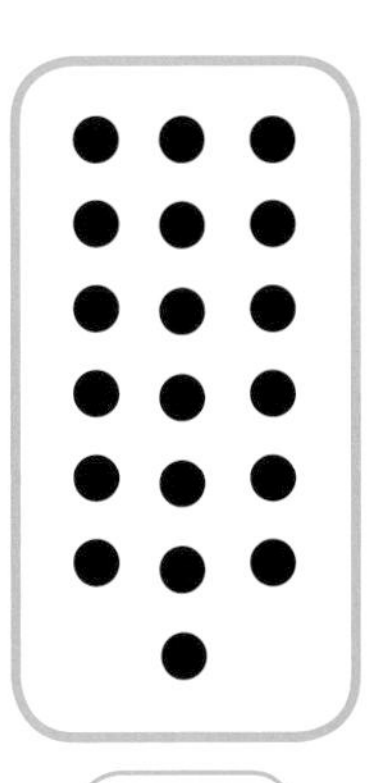

Practice the numbers

Connect the matching numbers, picture sets, and words.

20		sixteen
11		twelve
10		ten
18		eleven
12		twenty
16		eighteen

Draw a taller giraffe.

Draw a larger elephant.

Draw a longer snake.

Draw a thinner cat.

Compare length

Circle the longest vine.

Circle the skinniest bench.

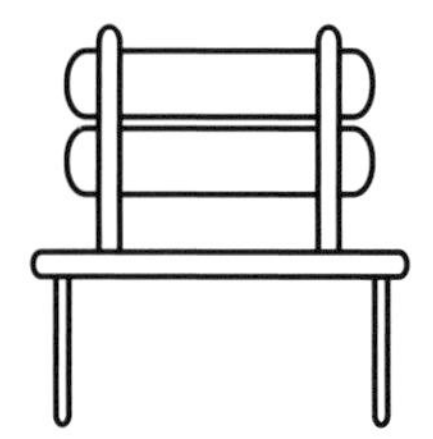 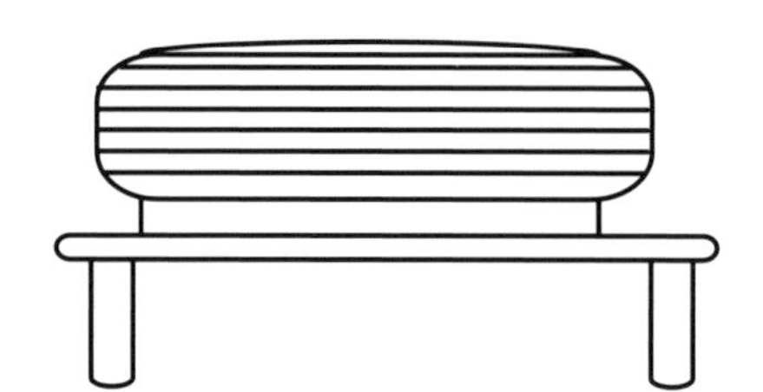 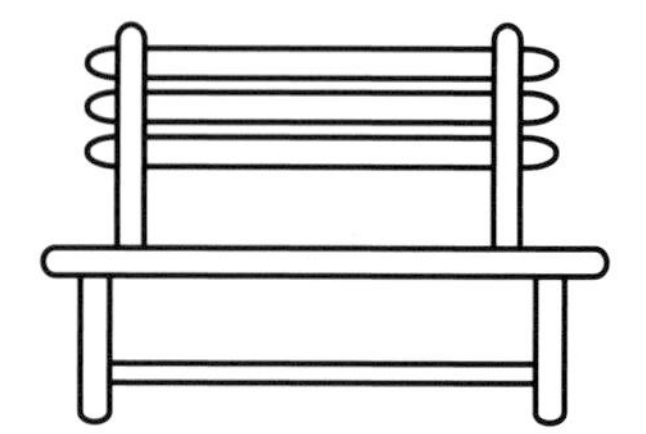

Circle the longest bush.

Circle the skinniest fence.

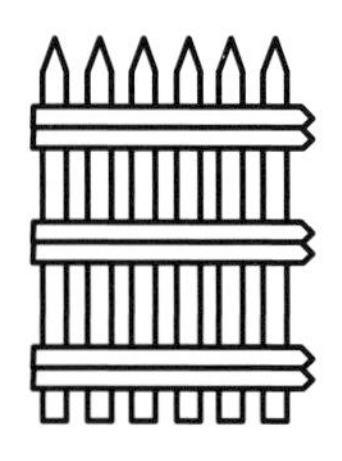   

Draw a circle...

next to the cat.

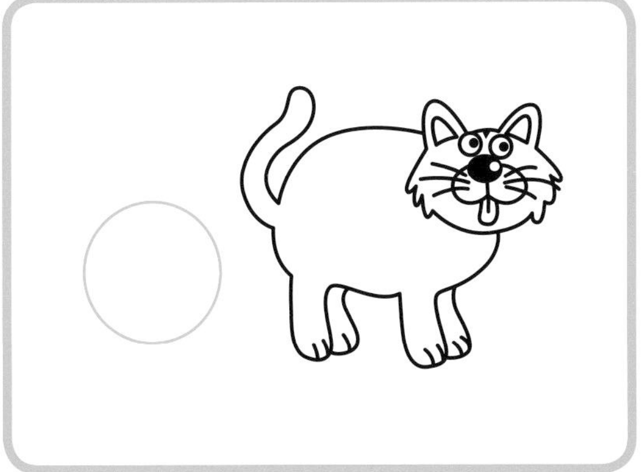

above the dog.

below the owl.

beneath the monkey.

beside the donkey.

on top of the cow.

More positions

What is in the middle of the park?

....

What is beneath the tree?

....

What is on the tree?

....

What is beside the pond?

....

What is in the pond?

....

Draw a dog next to the tree.

Write the days of the week in the right order.

Sunday | Monday | Thursday | Friday

Tuesday | Saturday | Wednesday

Sunday ....

....

What day comes before Tuesday?

....

What is two days after Monday?

....

How many days are there in a week?

....

How many days are there in two weeks?

....

The numbers below go from eleven to twenty, in order.
Write the missing numbers.

☐ 12 13 ☐ ☐

☐ 17 ☐ ☐ 20

How many are there in each group?

☐ mice ☐ chicks

Connect the shapes to their correct set.

4-sided Curved 3-sided

Write the answers.

12 – 2 = ☐ 17 – 7 = ☐ 20 – 2 = ☐

14 – 4 = ☐ 11 – 2 = ☐ 18 – 8 = ☐

Write 2 more than each number.

18 ☐ 12 ☐ 15 ☐ 11 ☐

Write 2 less than each number.

19 ☐ 14 ☐ 20 ☐ 17 ☐

Draw a snake that is shorter than the one shown.

Fill in the missing days.

Monday .... Wednesday ....

.... Sunday

Certificate

Congratulations to

....

for successfully finishing this book.

GOOD JOB!

You're a star.

Date

....

Answer Section with Parents' Notes

This book is designed for children who have the ability to count from zero up to 20, with a good understanding of the order and value of numbers.

Contents

By working through this book, your child will practice:

- reading, writing, and counting numbers to 20;
- the concept of same and different;
- the concept of more than and less than;
- the language and symbols of addition;
- the language and symbols of subtraction;
- the concept of simple number bonds;
- continuing simple sequences and patterns;
- recognizing simple 2-D shapes;
- classifying and sorting objects into sets;
- describing and comparing sizes and position.

How to help your child

It is very likely that many younger children will not be able to read some of the instructions in this book; that is understood by the author. Therefore, there is an expectation that parents, guardians, or helpers will work closely with children as they progress through this book, whether the child can read well or not. Both parents/helpers and children can gain a great deal from working together. Most children can understand math very well even if they are not yet able to read the language, so language should not be a reason to hold them back.

Wherever possible and necessary, try to give your children practical bits of equipment to help them, especially with the concept of adding and taking away. A collection of counters, buttons or similar small objects will be invaluable. As they become confident with the activities, the drawn objects may be sufficient.

Build your child's confidence by praise and encouragement. Celebrate their success.

4

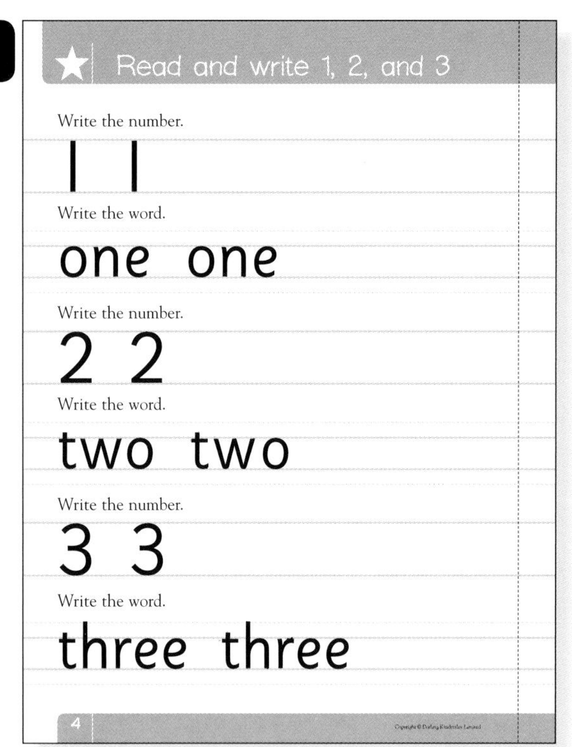

Read and write 1, 2, and 3

Write the number.

1 1

Write the word.

one one

Write the number.

2 2

Write the word.

two two

Write the number.

3 3

Write the word.

three three

4

Very young children need lots of practice at forming the correct shapes for the numbers. Whether they can form the number shapes well or not, they should recognize the numbers and have an understanding of the amount they represent.

5

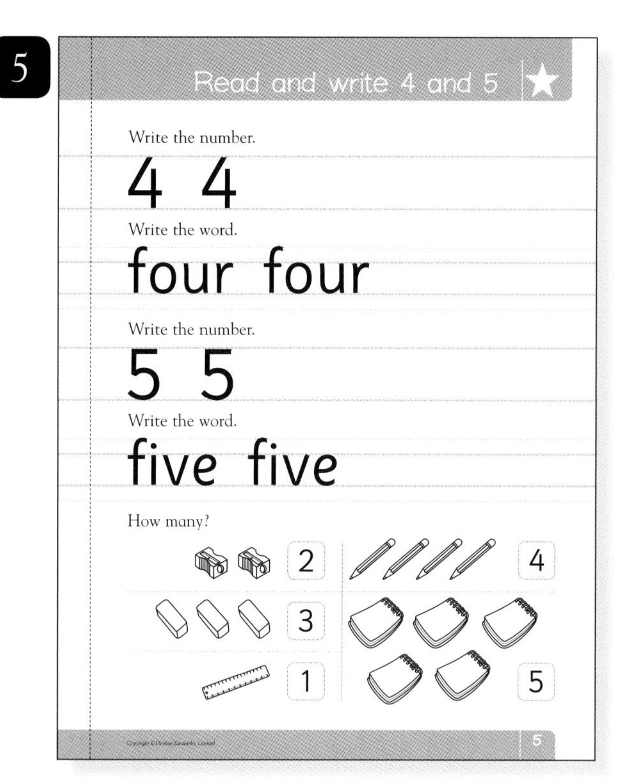

Read and write 4 and 5

Write the number.

4 4

Write the word.

four four

Write the number.

5 5

Write the word.

five five

How many?

2 4

3

1 5

5

Recognizing and being able to read the word that corresponds to each number may be difficult for the very youngest, but should be expected of many five year olds.

6

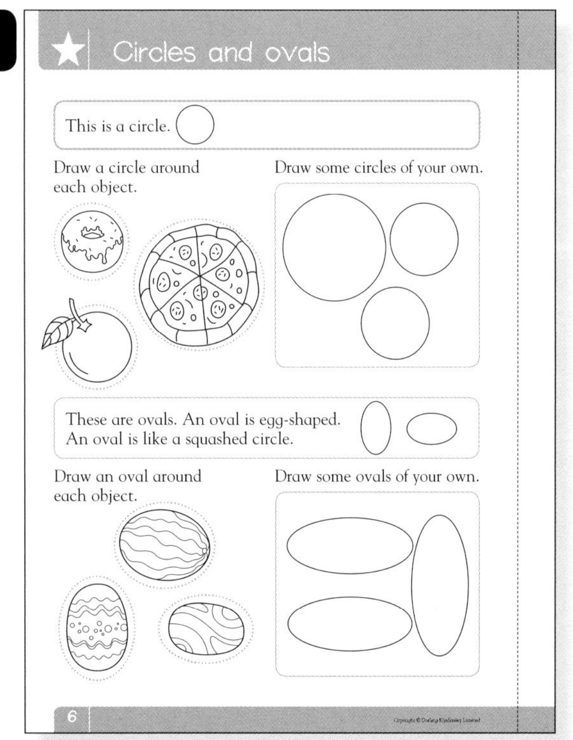

Circles and ovals

This is a circle.

Draw a circle around each object.

Draw some circles of your own.

These are ovals. An oval is egg-shaped. An oval is like a squashed circle.

Draw an oval around each object.

Draw some ovals of your own.

6

Children should be able to draw a circle fairly well. They could use coins to draw around. The oval is often described as being similar to an egg shape or a "squashed circle," which is fine as an introduction at this age.

7

The same

Circle the animal that is the same.

7

The phrase "the same as" is used to represent an equivalence of some sort. In these questions, children need to recognize an animal in the right column which "is the same as" the animals shown in the left column.

8

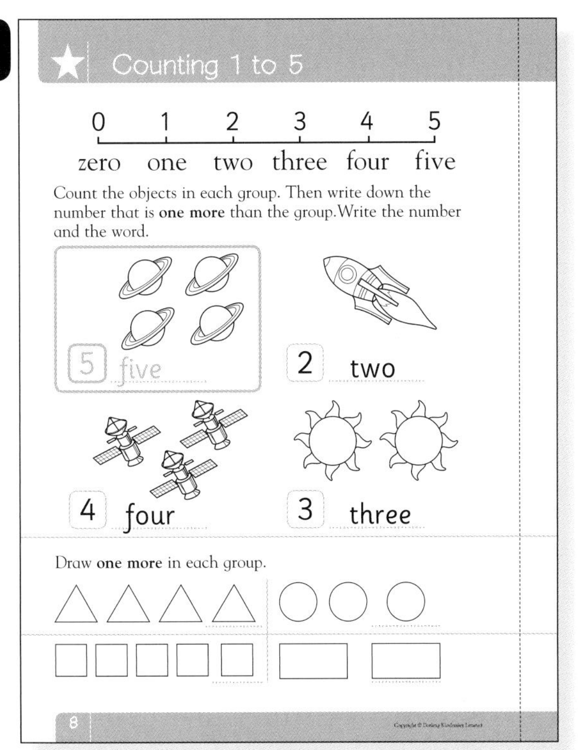
Counting 1 to 5

0 1 2 3 4 5
zero one two three four five

Count the objects in each group. Then write down the number that is **one more** than the group. Write the number and the word.

5 five

2 two

4 four

3 three

Draw **one more** in each group.

8 Copyright © Dorling Kindersley Limited

Number lines are commonly used with young children who should be encouraged to point to the numbers, and move along to find out what is "one more than." Basic shapes are also reinforced throughout the book.

9

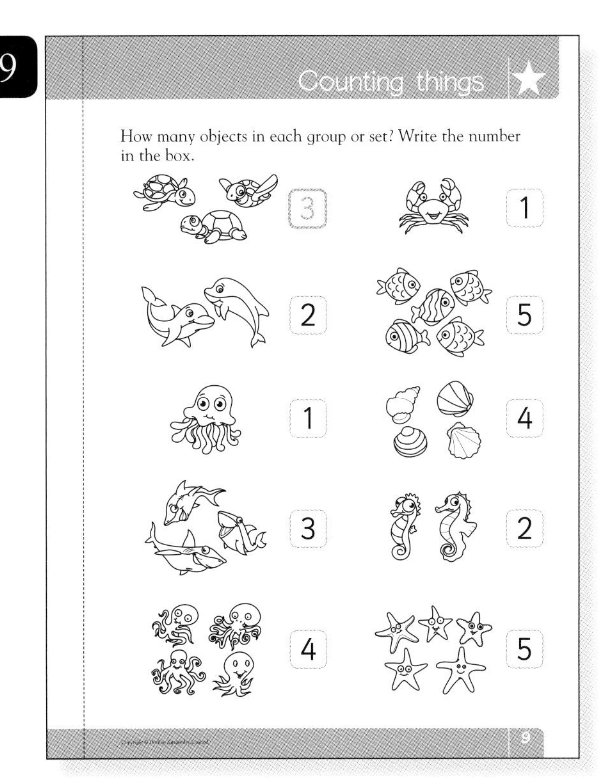
Counting things

How many objects in each group or set? Write the number in the box.

3 1

2 5

1 4

3 2

4 5

Copyright © Dorling Kindersley Limited 9

Children should be able to count up to five objects with confidence. To begin they might need to use a finger to actually touch each object as they count but they should be encouraged to recognize the number of objects just by looking, at least up to 10 or 12.

10

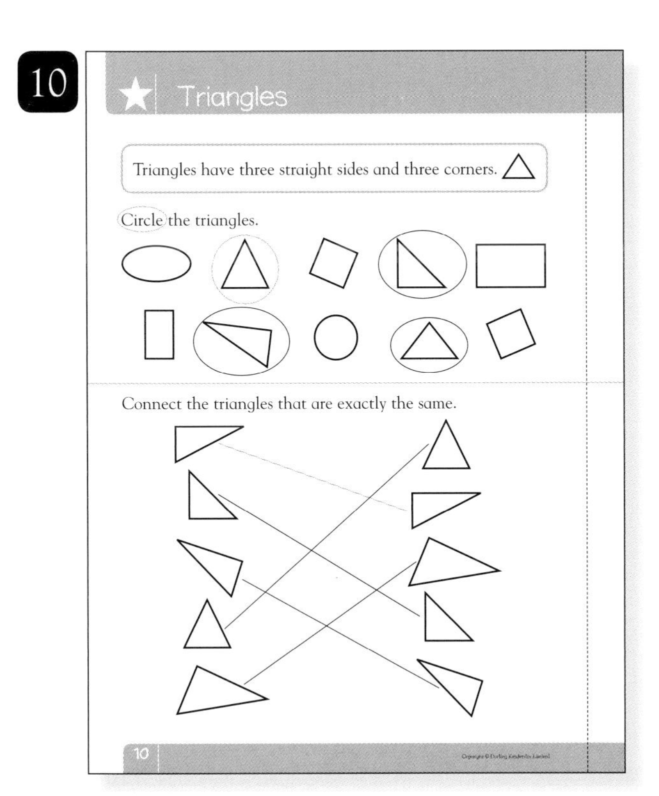
Triangles

Triangles have three straight sides and three corners.

Circle the triangles.

Connect the triangles that are exactly the same.

10 Copyright © Dorling Kindersley Limited

The main point of this page is for children to recognize the general name for a three-sided shape and examples of different types. It is not required for them to know the specific names and definitions at this stage.

11

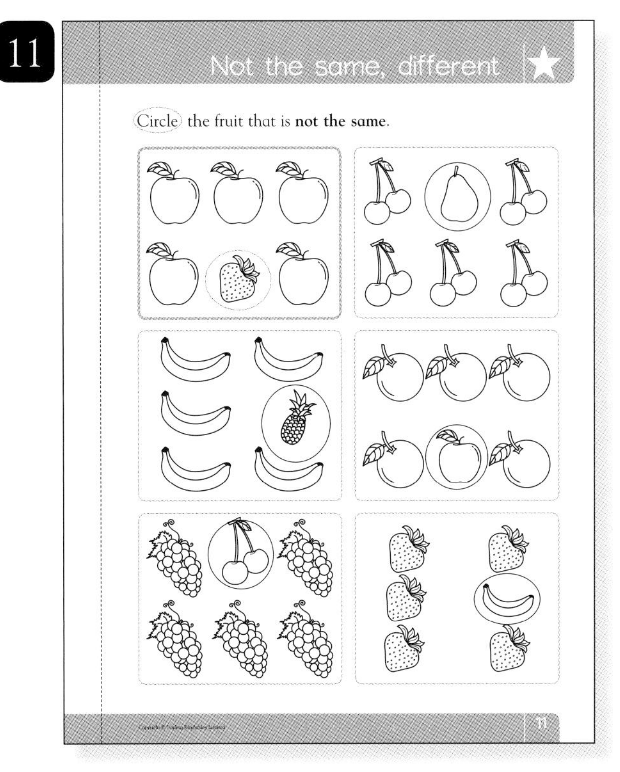
Not the same, different

Circle the fruit that is **not the same**.

Copyright © Dorling Kindersley Limited 11

Children should be able to recognize that one of the fruits in each group is not the same as the rest. The phrases "is not the same" and "different" can be used interchangeably at this age.

12

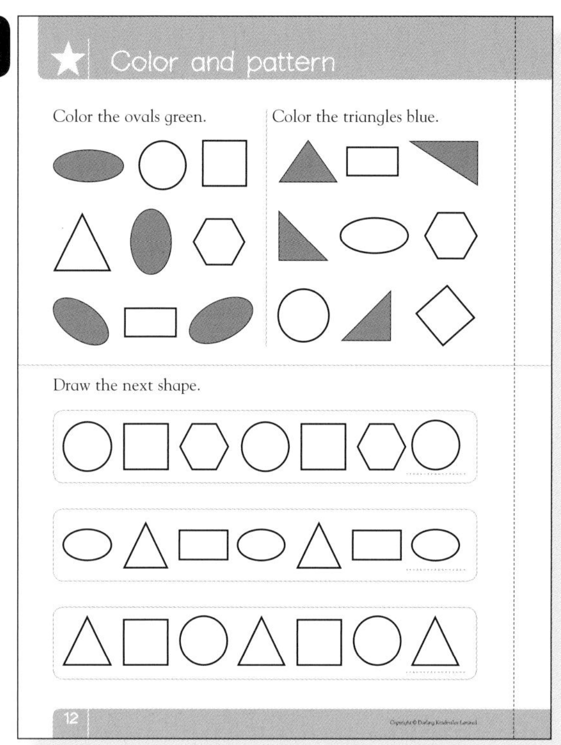

Color and pattern
Color the ovals green.
Color the triangles blue.
Draw the next shape.
12

This page helps children in two ways. First, children should recognize the simple patterns and be able to continue them. Secondly, the same shapes are used throughout and parents/helpers can reinforce previous learning by asking them to name the shapes in the patterns.

13

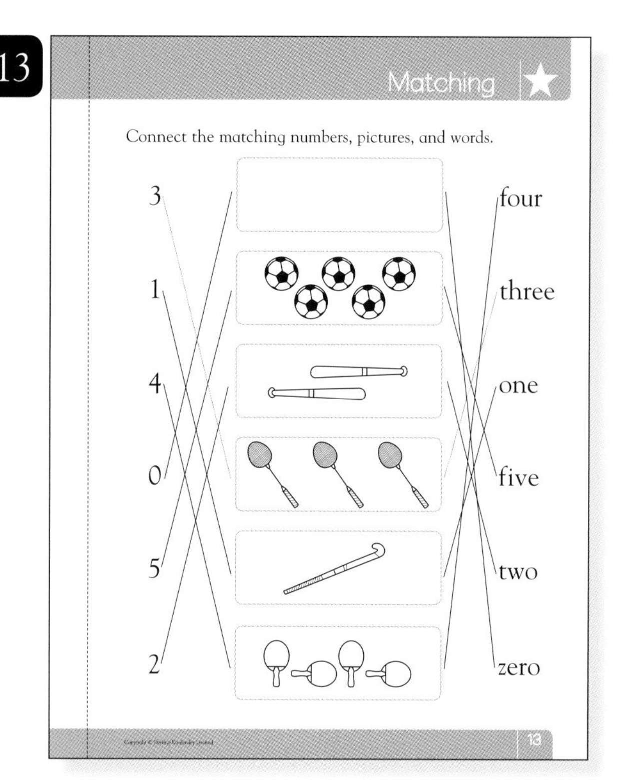

The work on this page will help children to match a number with its corresponding word as well as the number of objects.

14

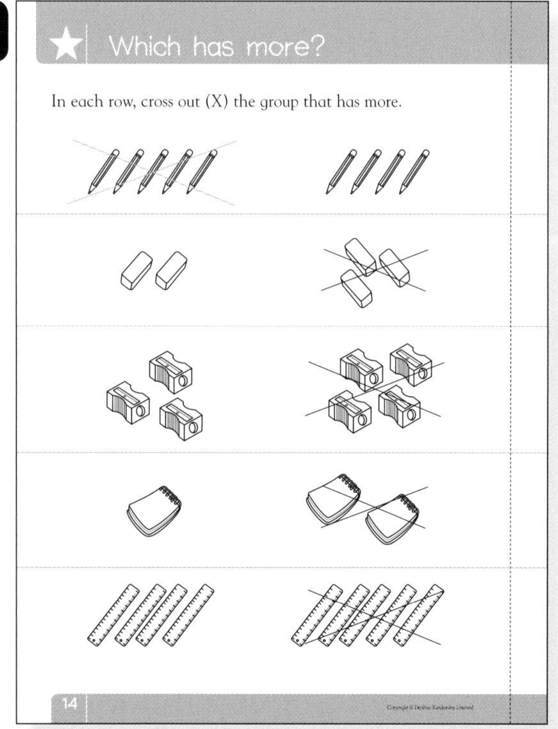

On this page, your child will need to count carefully. Ask your child to tell you which group has more objects. If the child is ready, you can also ask "How many more?"

15

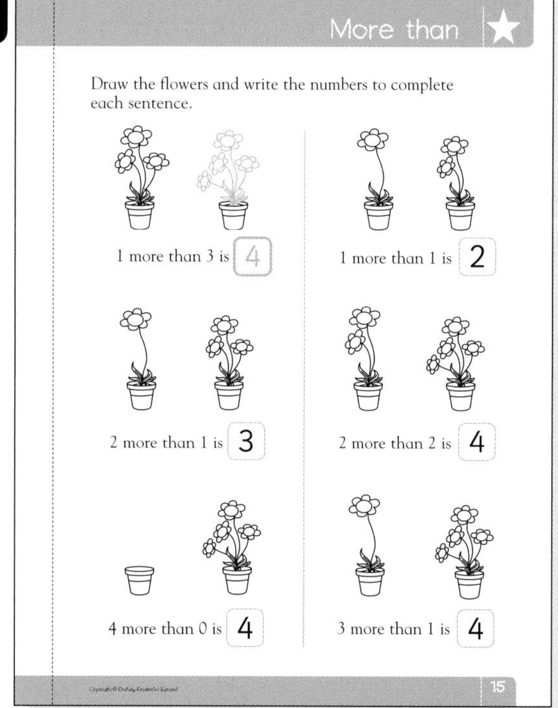

The words "1 more than" can be considered the beginnings of addition with the symbols "+" and "=" being introduced fairly soon. Draw a simple number line from 0 to 5 if it helps your child.

16

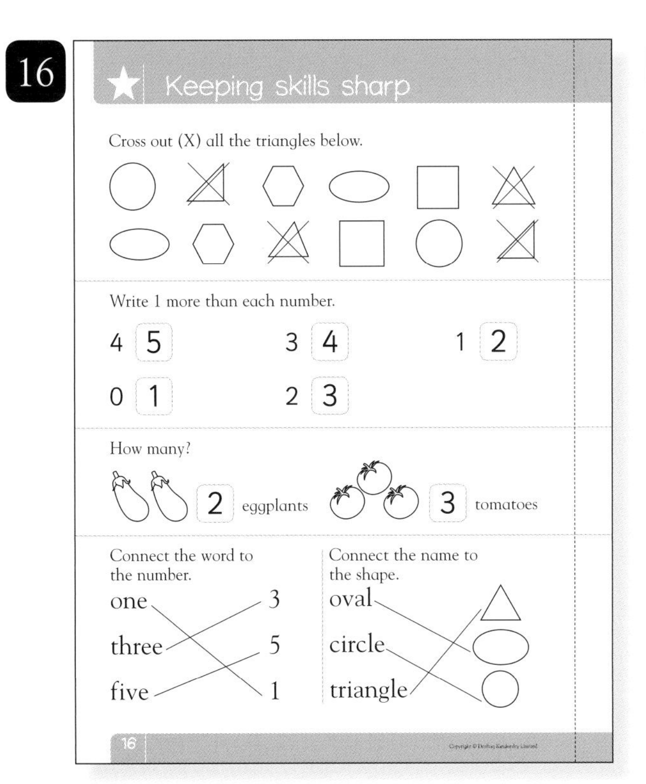

Keeping skills sharp

Cross out (X) all the triangles below.

Write 1 more than each number.

4 5 3 4 1 2

0 1 2 3

How many?

2 eggplants 3 tomatoes

Connect the word to the number.

one 3

three 5

five 1

Connect the name to the shape.

oval

circle

triangle

16 Copyright © Dorling Kindersley Limited

These pages review the work covered so far and should act as a reminder and a test of what has been learned. As ever, no pressure should be applied to children nor should a time limit be set.

17

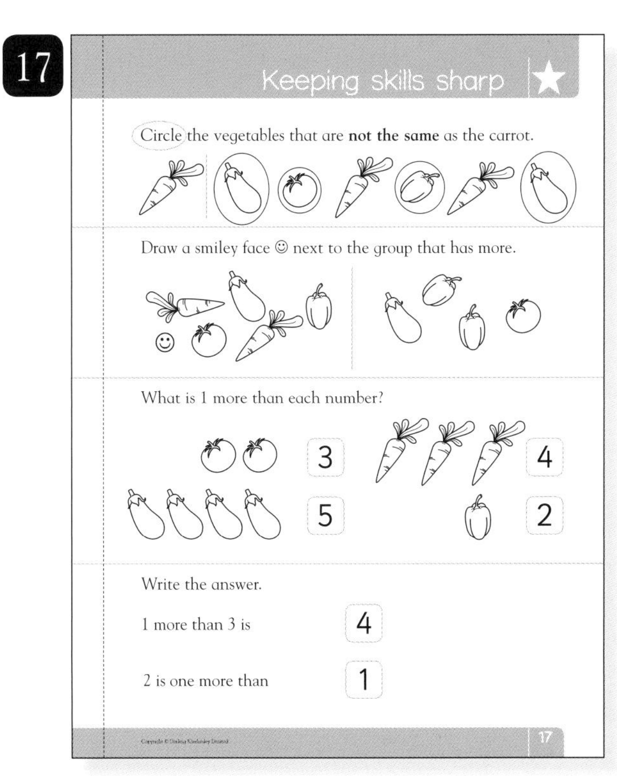

Keeping skills sharp

Circle the vegetables that are **not the same** as the carrot.

Draw a smiley face ☺ next to the group that has more.

What is 1 more than each number?

3 4

5 2

Write the answer.

1 more than 3 is 4

2 is one more than 1

Copyright © Dorling Kindersley Limited 17

Children should be encouraged to read the words, although they may need help in doing so.

18

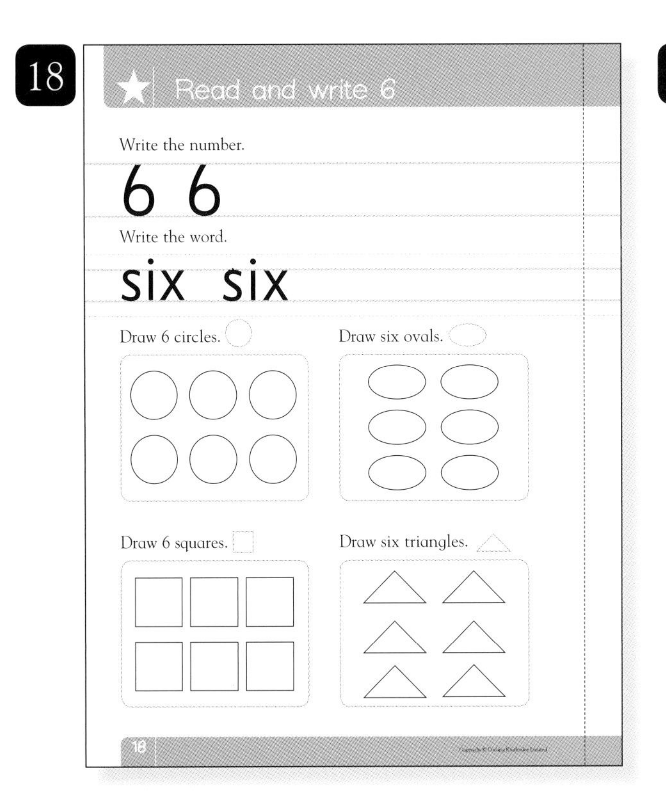

Read and write 6

Write the number.

6 6

Write the word.

six six

Draw 6 circles.

Draw six ovals.

Draw 6 squares.

Draw six triangles.

18 Copyright © Dorling Kindersley Limited

It is very likely young children will recognize the shapes of the numbers 6 and 7 but will still need practice in their formation.

19

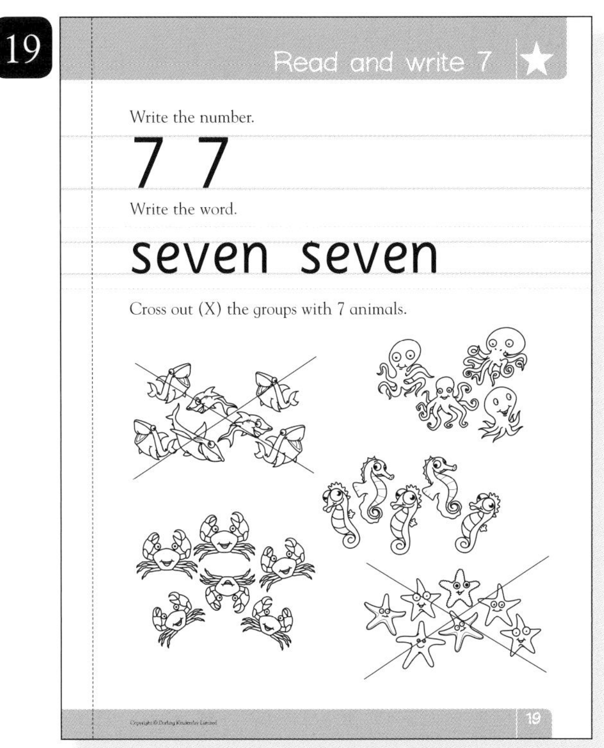

Read and write 7

Write the number.

7 7

Write the word.

seven seven

Cross out (X) the groups with 7 animals.

Copyright © Dorling Kindersley Limited 19

As with all the other numbers, the sooner children recognize the number and associate it with the corresponding word the better.

20

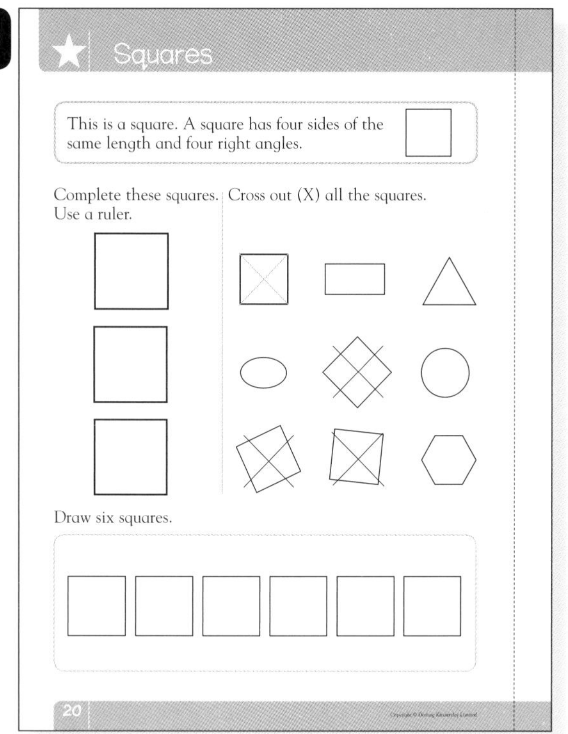
Squares

This is a square. A square has four sides of the same length and four right angles.

Complete these squares. Use a ruler.

Cross out (X) all the squares.

Draw six squares.

20

The square is one in a series of special shapes children need to learn. The definition of a square includes the term "four right angles." Although a knowledge of right angles would not normally have been taught by this age, it would be helpful if the parent/helper explains the term.

21

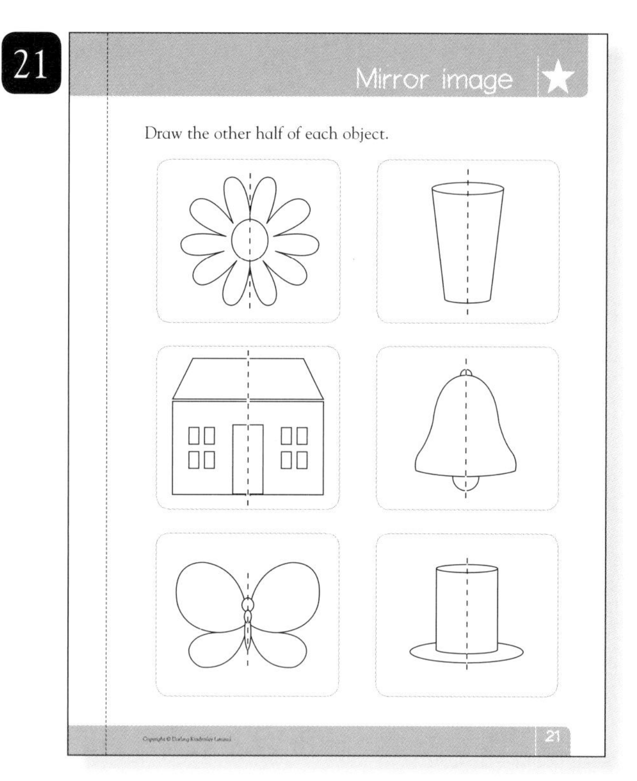
Mirror image

Draw the other half of each object.

21

Children are likely to be familiar with words such as "reflection" and should find this page straightforward and enjoyable. Have a small mirror at hand so children can check their drawing by placing it along the dotted line of symmetry.

22

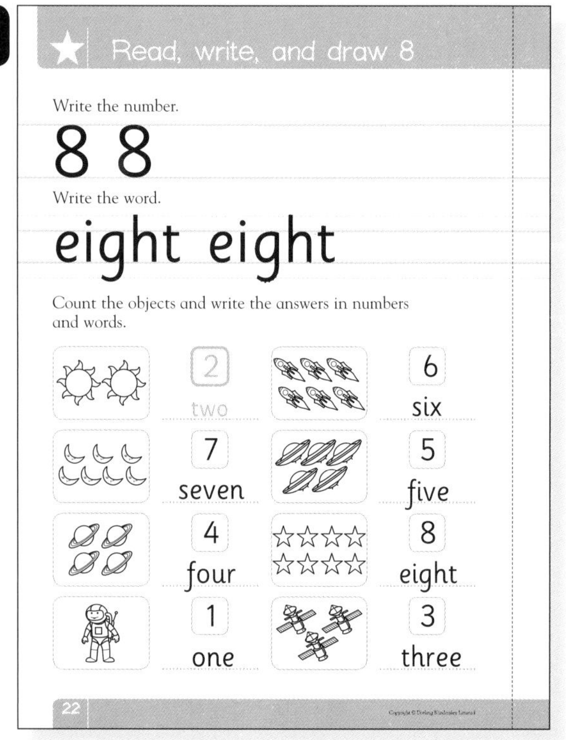
Read, write, and draw 8

Write the number.

8 8

Write the word.

eight eight

Count the objects and write the answers in numbers and words.

	2 two		6 six
	7 seven		5 five
	4 four		8 eight
	1 one		3 three

22

If children need extra practice writing any of the numbers from 0 to 9, allow them time to do this on a lined piece of paper.

23

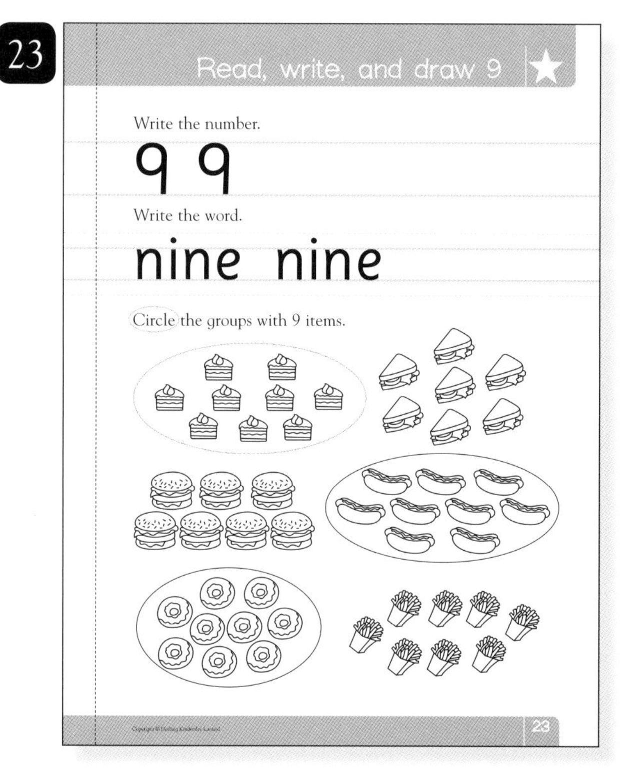
Read, write, and draw 9

Write the number.

9 9

Write the word.

nine nine

Circle the groups with 9 items.

23

Emphasis is given to recognizing number shapes and the corresponding number words to improve childen's math vocabulary throughout this book.

24

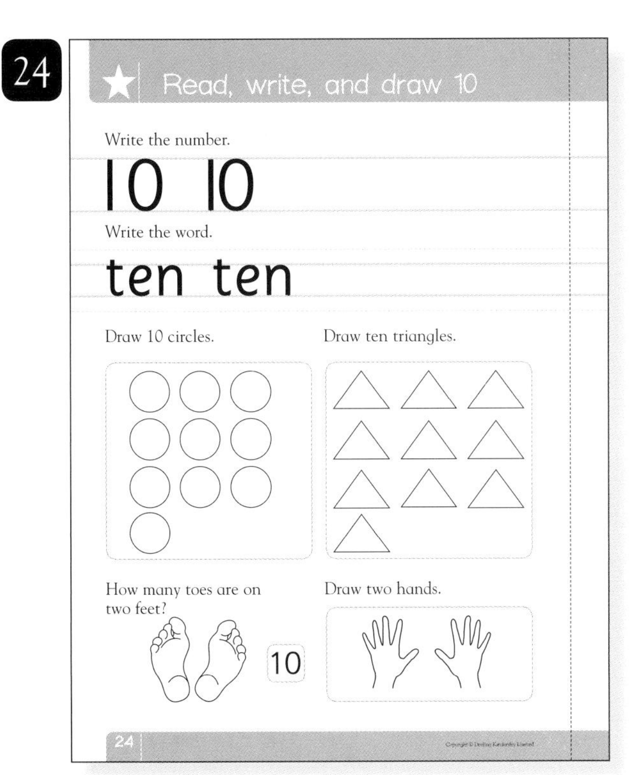

Read, write, and draw 10

Write the number.

10 10

Write the word.

ten ten

Draw 10 circles. Draw ten triangles.

How many toes are on two feet? 10

Draw two hands.

24 Copyright © Dorling Kindersley Limited

The drawing exercises on this page are only intended to help children count to ten and keep a mental note as they draw. It is not meant for them to spend ages carefully drawing each shape.

25

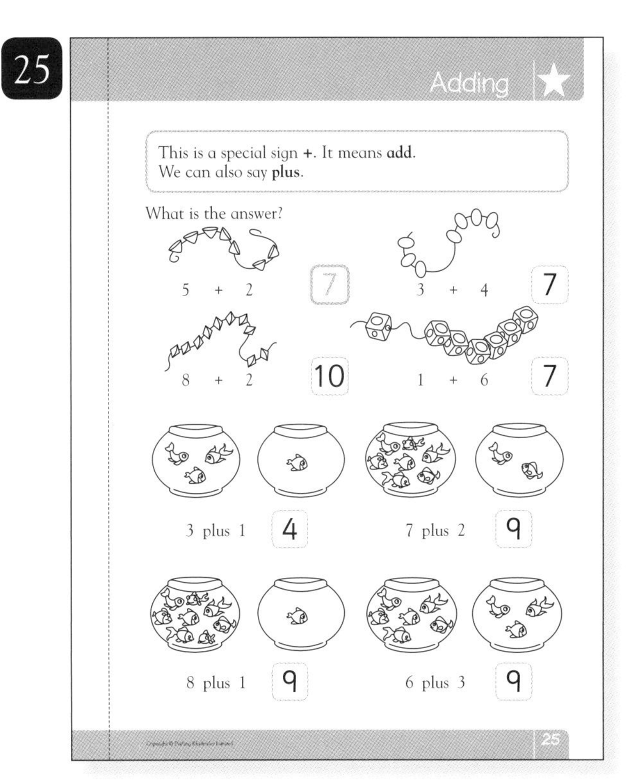

Adding

This is a special sign **+**. It means **add**. We can also say **plus**.

What is the answer?

5 + 2 = 7

3 + 4 = 7

8 + 2 = 10

1 + 6 = 7

3 plus 1 = 4

7 plus 2 = 9

8 plus 1 = 9

6 plus 3 = 9

Copyright © Dorling Kindersley Limited 25

This page introduces the plus "+" sign. Children will need to be able to read it, write it, and understand its implications. It is important they learn that the operation of adding can be shown through different phrases such as "add," "plus," "increase" or "increase by," or "more than."

26

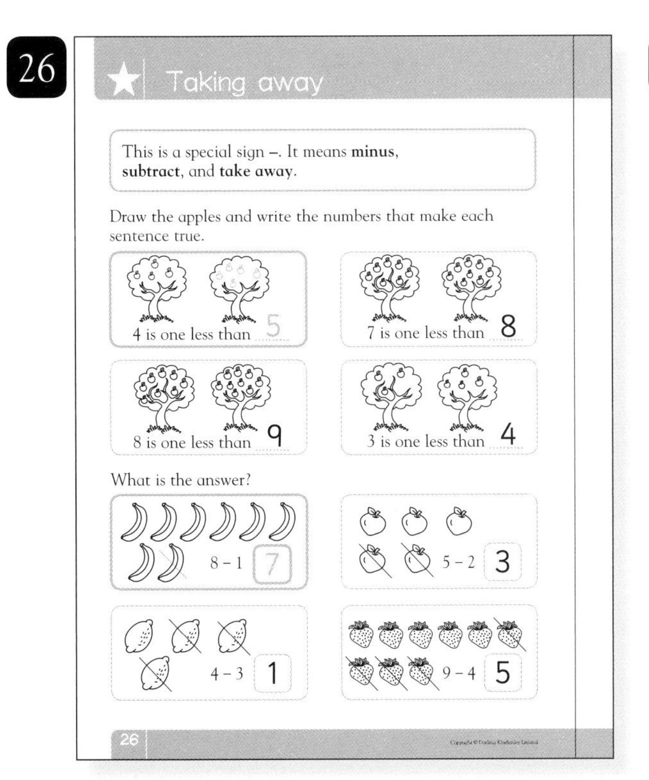

Taking away

This is a special sign –. It means **minus**, **subtract**, and **take away**.

Draw the apples and write the numbers that make each sentence true.

4 is one less than 5

7 is one less than 8

8 is one less than 9

3 is one less than 4

What is the answer?

8 – 1 = 7

5 – 2 = 3

4 – 3 = 1

9 – 4 = 5

26 Copyright © Dorling Kindersley Limited

This page introduces the minus "–" sign. Children should know various ways of saying the operation of subtraction such as "reduce" or "reduce by," "take away," "less than" etc.

27

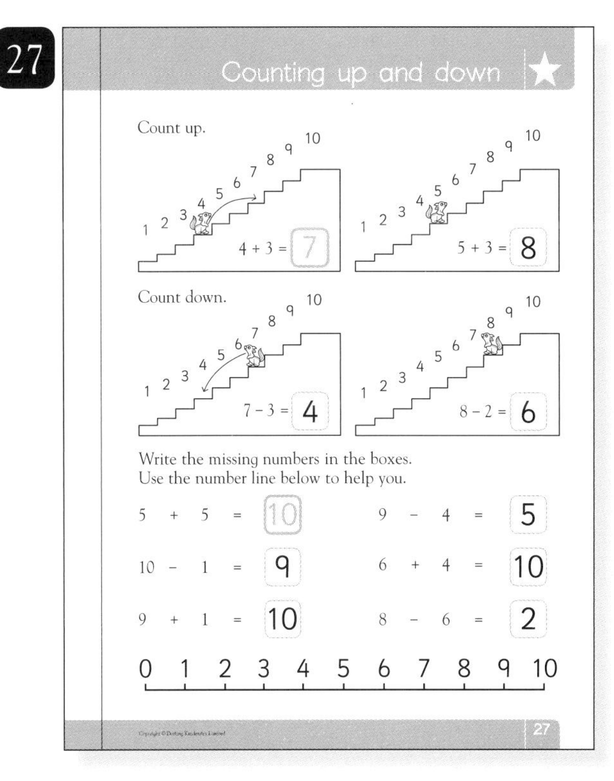

Counting up and down

Count up.

4 + 3 = 7

5 + 3 = 8

Count down.

7 – 3 = 4

8 – 2 = 6

Write the missing numbers in the boxes. Use the number line below to help you.

5 + 5 = 10

9 – 4 = 5

10 – 1 = 9

6 + 4 = 10

9 + 1 = 10

8 – 6 = 2

0 1 2 3 4 5 6 7 8 9 10

Copyright © Dorling Kindersley Limited 27

This page introduces the special "=" sign, which will become more important as children move through school. Encourage them to look carefully at each question before answering it, as they may add instead of subtract or vice versa.

28

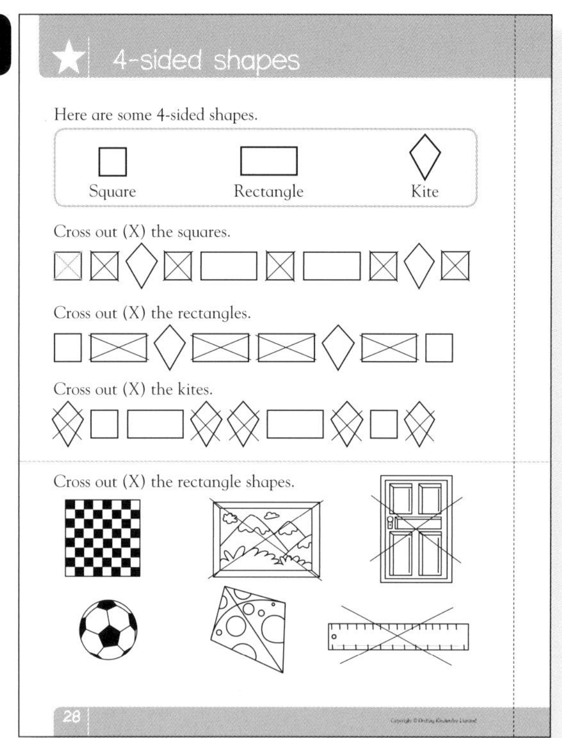

4-sided shapes
Here are some 4-sided shapes.
Square
Rectangle
Kite
Cross out (X) the squares.
Cross out (X) the rectangles.
Cross out (X) the kites.
Cross out (X) the rectangle shapes.
28

Children should notice similarities between these shapes like having four straight sides. More importantly, children should notice the differences, like having equal sides or right angles.

Dot-to-dot

29

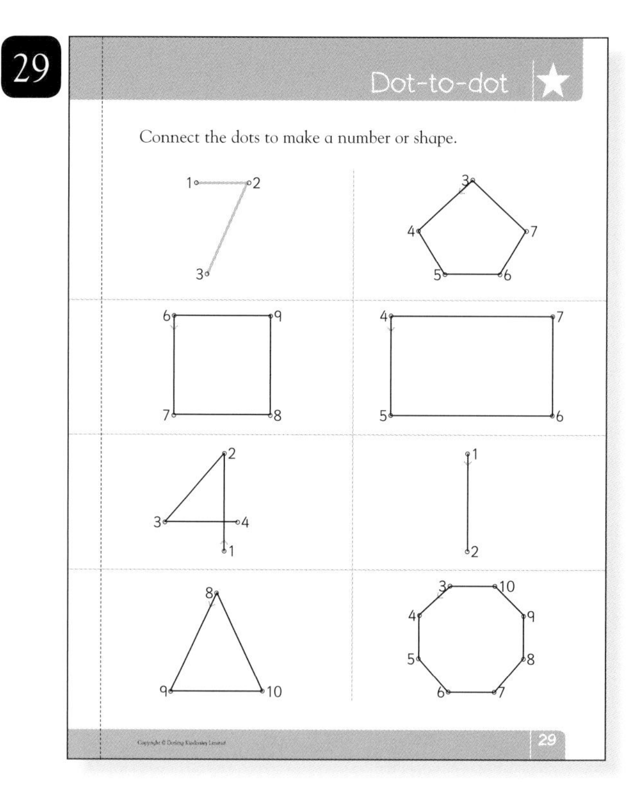

This page reviews number order.

30

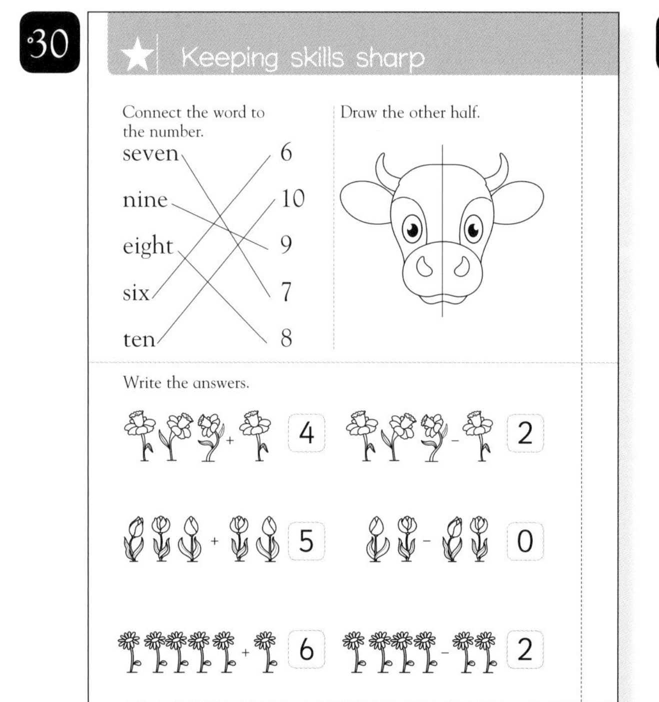

This test will check how well previous pages have been learned.

Four add four is 8
Nine plus one is 10
Eight plus one is 9
Two add three is 5

31

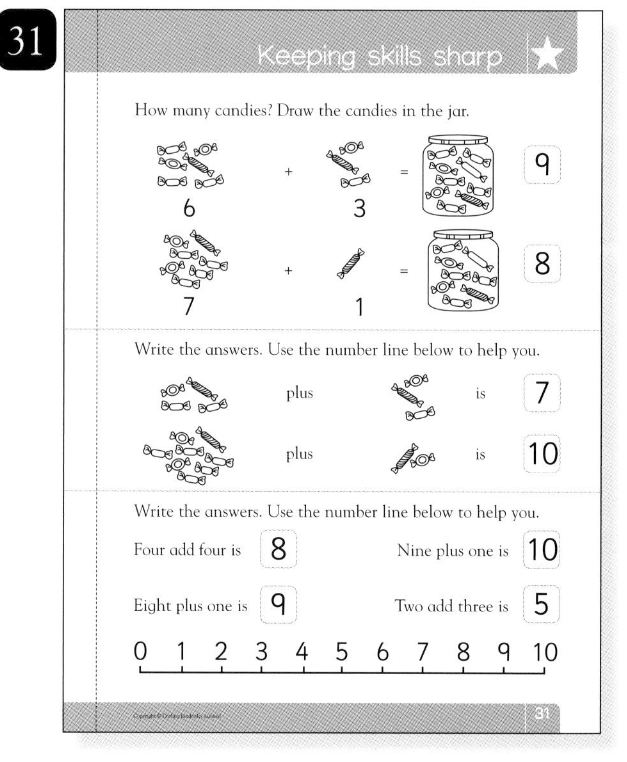

Very young children may need help with the words in the last problem.

32

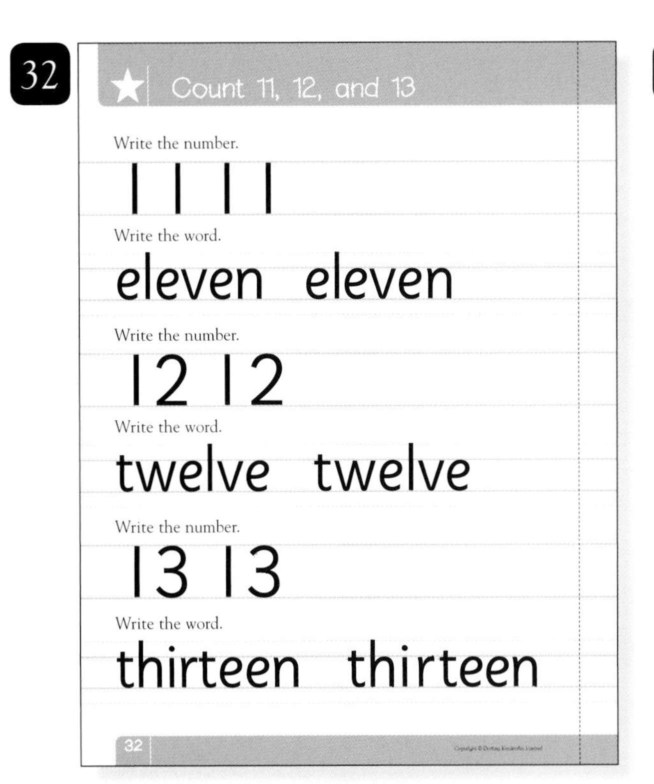

Count 11, 12, and 13
Write the number.
11 11
Write the word.
eleven eleven
Write the number.
12 12
Write the word.
twelve twelve
Write the number.
13 13
Write the word.
thirteen thirteen
32

As children develop their mathematical understanding of numbers they will learn about larger numbers.

33

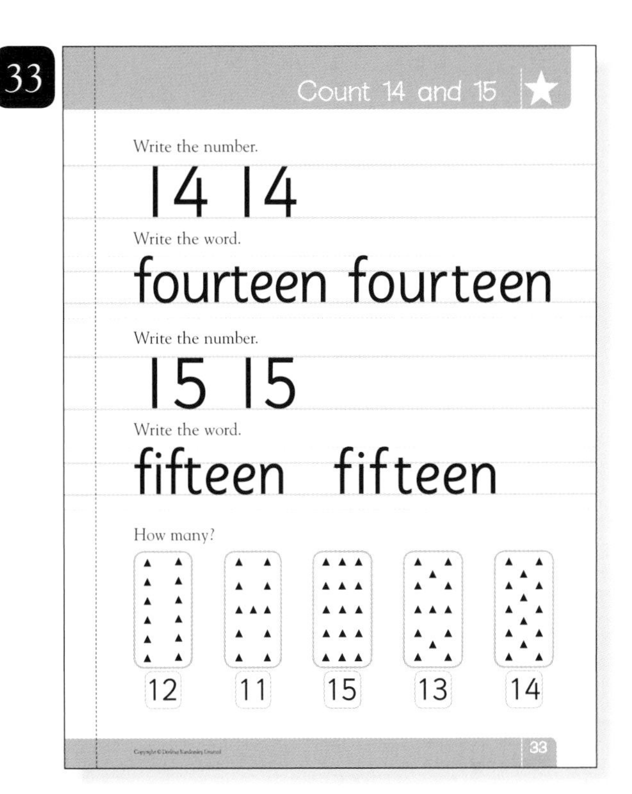

Count 14 and 15
Write the number.
14 14
Write the word.
fourteen fourteen
Write the number.
15 15
Write the word.
fifteen fifteen
How many?
12
11
15
13
14
33

This page provides extra practice with larger numbers.

34

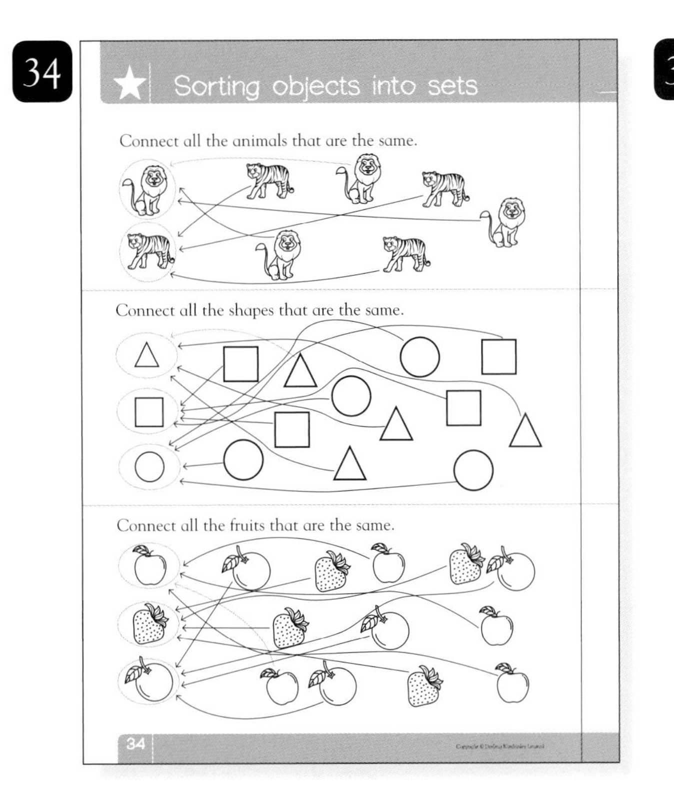

Sorting objects into sets
Connect all the animals that are the same.
Connect all the shapes that are the same.
Connect all the fruits that are the same.
34

Sorting objects into sets helps to develop logical thinking. Parents/helpers can ask children why they have made a particular selection and encourage them to talk about the attributes of the objects in the sets.

35

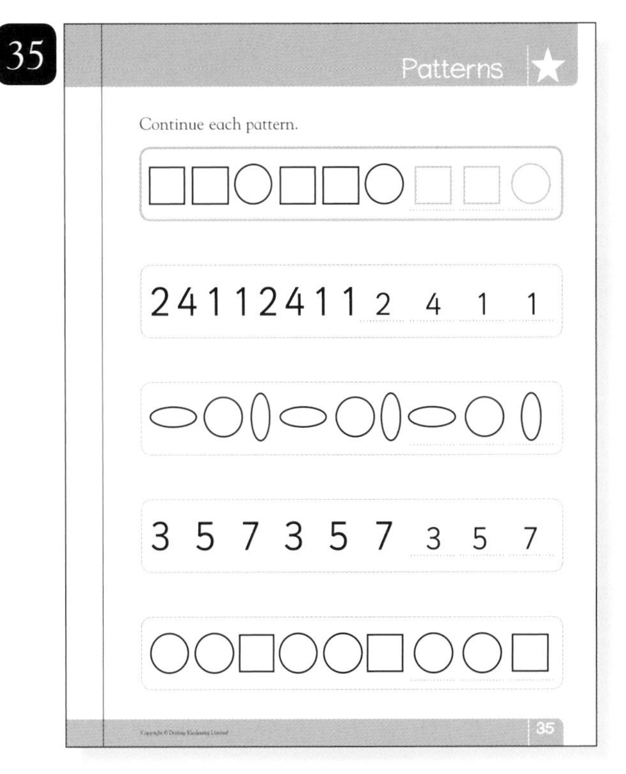

Patterns
Continue each pattern.
2 4 1 1 2 4 1 1 2 4 1 1
3 5 7 3 5 7 3 5 7
35

As with sorting objects, children should be recognizing attributes of groups and objects, and using this knowledge to continue the patterns.

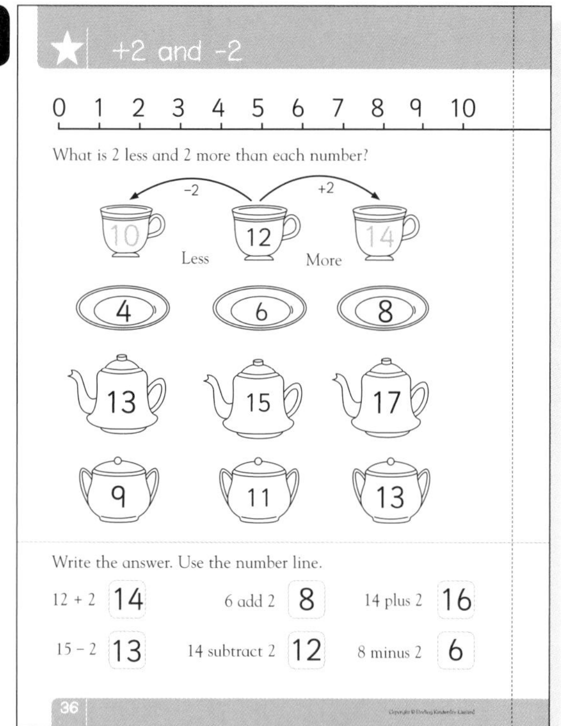

Pages 36–37 contain addition and subtraction questions. The number line should be useful but encourage children to work without it (by covering it) if they seem confident.

37

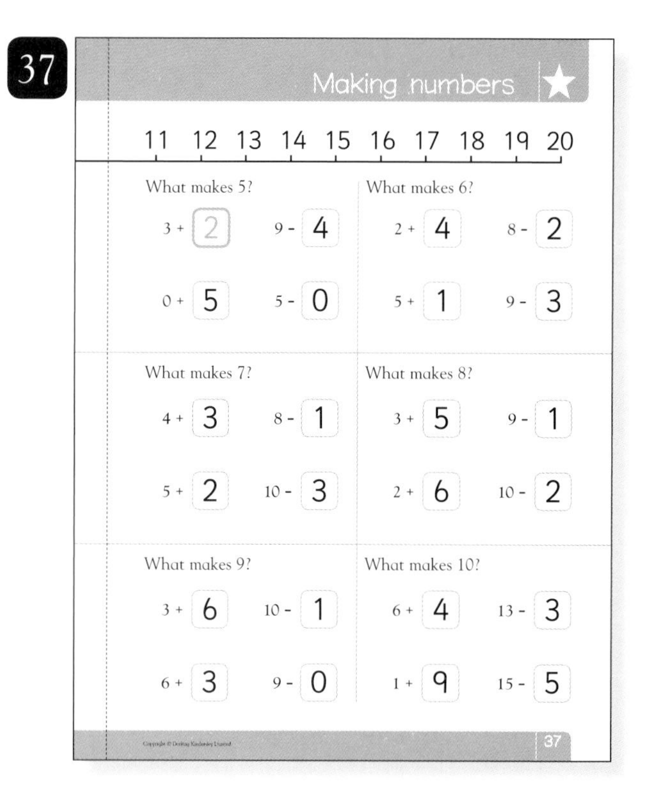

38

Count 16, 17, and 18

Write the number.

16 16

Write the word.

sixteen sixteen

Write the number.

17 17

Write the word.

seventeen seventeen

Write the number.

18 18

Write the word.

eighteen eighteen

38

39

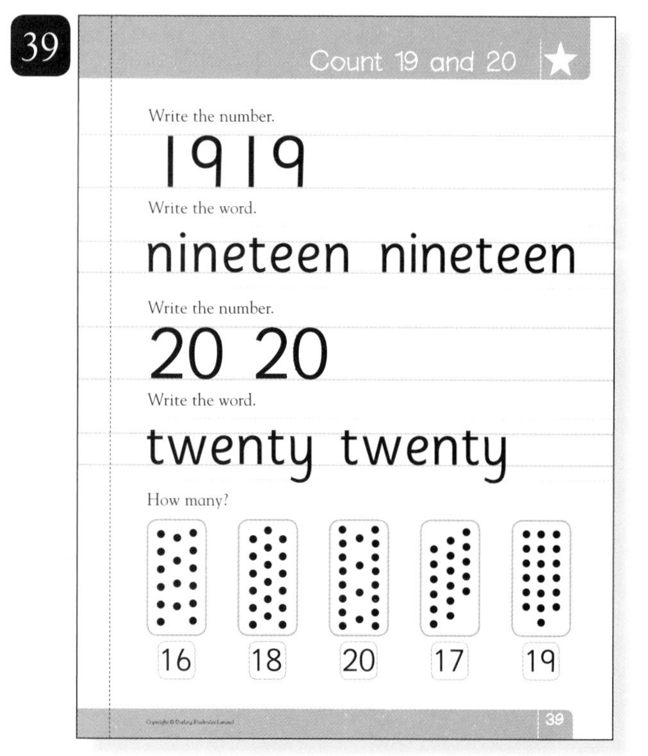

Children can mark each dot with a line or number as it is counted. This is time consuming, but can be helpful when counting higher than 10.

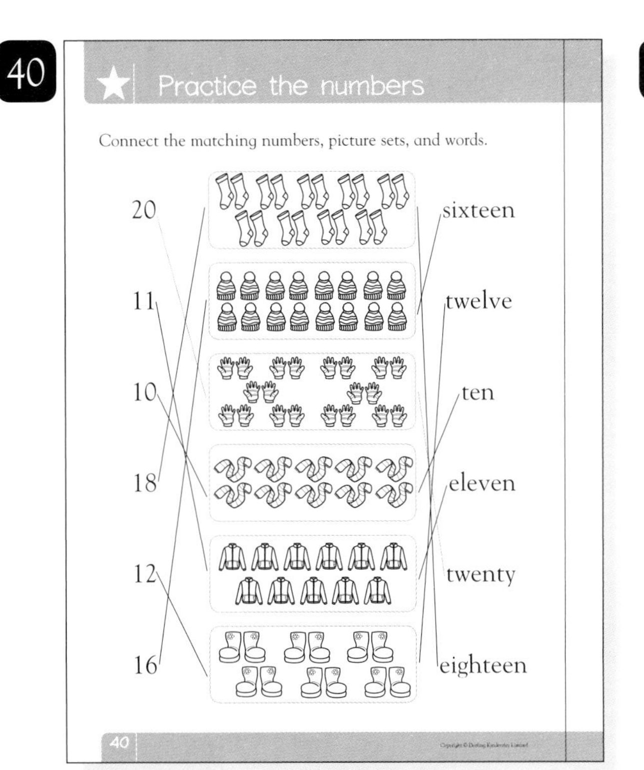

This page reviews numbers from 10 to 20. The numbers are shown as figures, in sets, and as words.

Children need to know words that relate to size and position, such as "behind" and "larger."

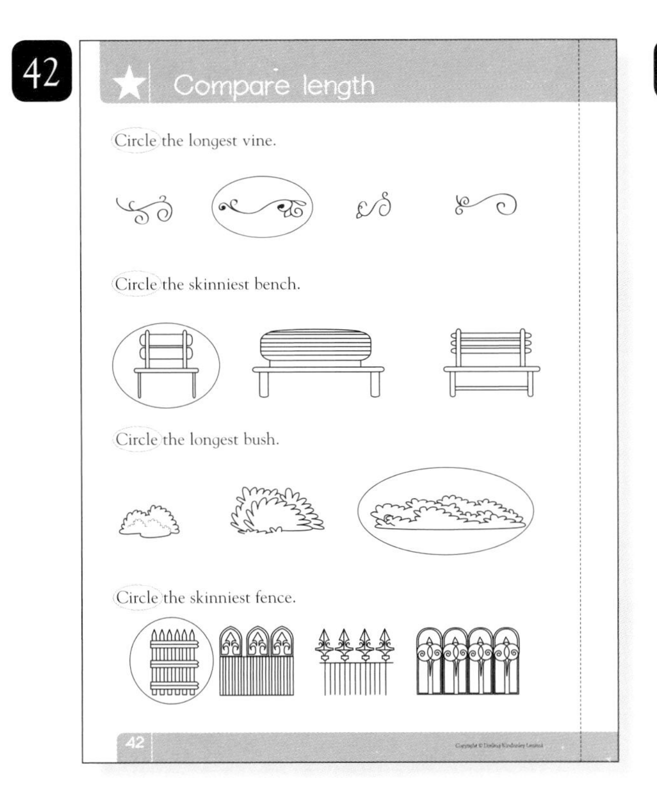

42
Compare length
Circle the longest vine.
Circle the skinniest bench.
Circle the longest bush.
Circle the skinniest fence.
42

This page practices words to do with length.

Ask children to point out the position words on this page as well. Ask them if they know the opposite position or can identify them on this page.

44

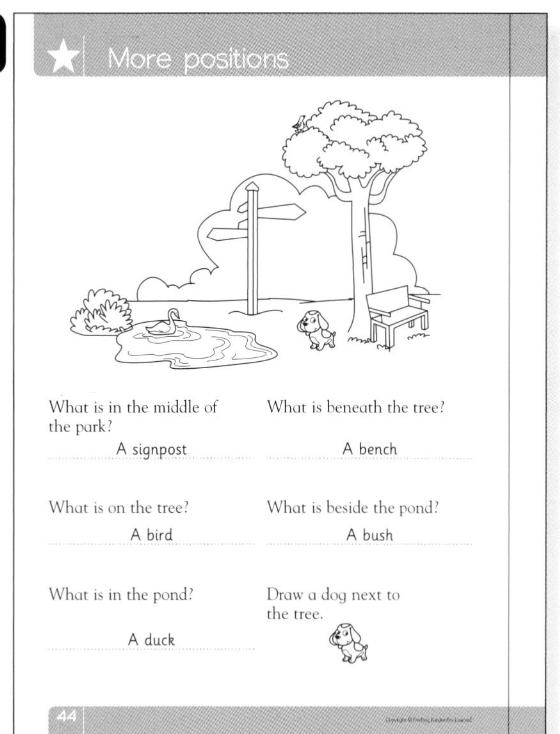

More positions

What is in the middle of the park? A signpost

What is beneath the tree? A bench

What is on the tree? A bird

What is beside the pond? A bush

What is in the pond? A duck

Draw a dog next to the tree.

Take opportunities to use position words in real-life situations with children.

45

Days of the week

Write the days of the week in the right order.

Sunday Monday Thursday Friday

Tuesday Saturday Wednesday

Sunday Monday Tuesday Wednesday

Thursday Friday Saturday

What day comes before Tuesday?

Monday

What is two days after Monday?

Wednesday

How many days are there in a week?

Seven

How many days are there in two weeks?

Fourteen

Children should know the days of the week by now and this page gives them the opportunity to read the names and talk with parents/helpers about the right order of days. Encourage your child to learn how to spell the words too.

46

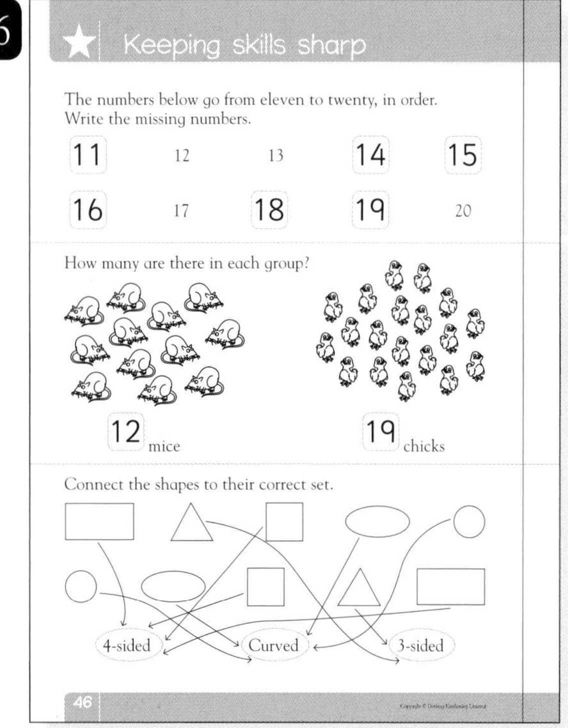

Keeping skills sharp

The numbers below go from eleven to twenty, in order. Write the missing numbers.

11 12 13 14 15

16 17 18 19 20

How many are there in each group?

12 mice 19 chicks

Connect the shapes to their correct set.

4-sided Curved 3-sided

These are the final revision questions in the book. They should provide a good indication of the success children have had with the work in this book.

47

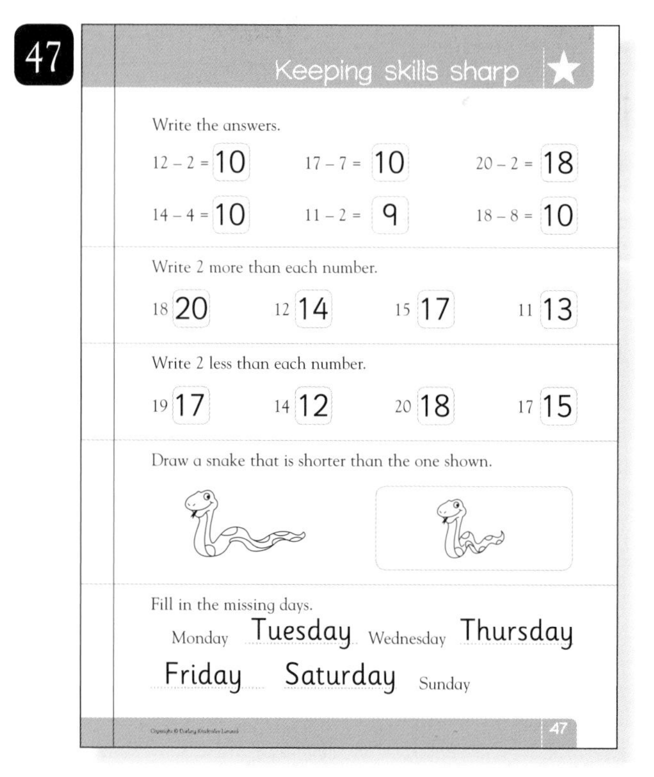

Keeping skills sharp

Write the answers.

12 – 2 = 10 17 – 7 = 10 20 – 2 = 18

14 – 4 = 10 11 – 2 = 9 18 – 8 = 10

Write 2 more than each number.

18 20 12 14 15 17 11 13

Write 2 less than each number.

19 17 14 12 20 18 17 15

Draw a snake that is shorter than the one shown.

Fill in the missing days.

Monday Tuesday Wednesday Thursday

Friday Saturday Sunday

The bumper *Math Made Easy* workbooks provide more practice worksheets.